The Zen of the Director

The Zen
of the Director

Mind and Process
for the Filmmaker

Peter Markham

Sticking Place Books
New York

Also by Peter Markham

The Art of the Filmmaker:
The Practical Aesthetics of the Screen

What's the Story? The Director Meets Their Screenplay:
An Essential Guide for Directors and Writer-Directors

© Sticking Place Books 2025
© Peter Markham

www.stickingplacebooks.com

ISBN 979-8-89976-038-9

For my students,
who have become my teachers.

CONTENTS

INTRODUCTION

If my first book, *What's the Story?*, was about the director and the narrative, and my second, *The Art of the Filmmaker,* was about the director and the screen, this third, *The Zen of the Director*, is about the director and their self.

Far from offering a purely introspective focus, this book takes a broad look at how the director might understand both their interior and exterior processes. In what areas lie the decisions they need to take? When do they need to take them? What prompts the director's decision-making? Is their response to the material at hand founded in helpful inner resources or are other perhaps hidden agendas playing out—ones that may have little or nothing to do with the film the director is making?

Similarly, in their prep of the film, which I like to call the *formulation*, and later, on set and in post-production, and in the director's collaboration with their creative team, what factors are brought to bear? Which might be relevant and functional, which irrelevant and dysfunctional?

What is the place of ego in all of this, and can the director find ways of overcoming its often toxic influence?

What defensive barricades might the director be putting up? Against elements of their material they might be uncomfortable with? Against ideas and insights better than their own? Against fresh ways of thinking? Against creative risk? Against challenges they might prefer not to face?

Further, what are the many voices that might come into play? From within, from without? What, exactly, might these be and how might the filmmaker recognize them? How might they assess their value and either make use of them or guard against the unhelpful, even damaging ones?

These topics lead us to practical considerations for the director—and while every director differs from their peers, the questions explored in this book are, I believe, largely universal.

In taking Zen as a key to this exploration, the reader need not fear that fanciful metaphysics will obscure this book's central concern: the director's work on the self, and consequently on their film. Quite the opposite, in fact. The simplicity and practice of Zen, far from being fanciful but to the contrary, long proven through generations, can illuminate the contemporary task of filmmaking, which to many may seem far removed from such an ancient discipline.

Nor should readers—most of whom, like me, may not be practicing Buddhists—feel daunted by what they might perceive as an arcane notion. Zen, at its core, embodies simple, fundamental principles accessible to all. Many of these can prove invaluable to the director in developing and refining self-awareness as a filmmaker—one attuned to their material, their craft, and their collaboration with others: cast, crew, and creative partners alike.

In each of this book's chapters, these aspects of Zen are related to the craft and practice of directing. Where do they offer insight, and where might they seem to stand in tension with elements of the director's multifaceted vocation?

If this might seem a distraction from the exacting, pressured, and all too vulnerable pursuit of the film-maker, my original inspiration for this book came not from Zen but from the words of one of the great masters of cinema:

Il ne s'agit pas de diriger quelqu'un, mais de se diriger soi-même.

The point is not to direct someone, but to direct one's self.

Robert Bresson. *Notes on the Cinematograph*.

Over the years, as I have returned again and again to this short book, different sentences have struck me at different moments. But the profound, seminal truth of this one, above all, is something I should have understood and embraced far earlier. It is not confined to the filmmaker; it applies equally to the awareness of all of us as we go about our lives.

It might, I suggest, be related to what I am calling The Zen of the Director.

If some aspects of Zen may seem less directly relevant, I hope the core of this book serves as a pointer toward more clearly perceiving the symbiosis of inner and outer activity that Bresson evokes. This partnership between psyche and world is one that the film director—no less than anyone else, and with their dual concern for individual creative invention and collaboration with fellow filmmakers—must learn to appreciate, attend to, and, through genuine understanding, draw upon for its many-sided rewards.

Martin Scorsese offers us this:

There are no manuals, no shortcuts, no secrets.

Like my first two books, this one is in no way intended as any such definitive "manual" in the sense many others are. Nor is it a "how to" treatise. It does not so much instruct the reader in what to know as explore possible ways of discovering, thinking about, and reflecting on the director's mindsets, attitudes, and approaches—on their work and play, within and without—throughout the filmmaking process.

In short, this is a book that through a Zen perspective looks in at the soul of the director as they go about their work and considers how that interiority might inform their navigation of their self, their material, and their collaboration with their creative team.

If not an academic work nor the ministrations of a lifestyle guru, if not a "how-to" tract, it is equally not a self-help book. My intention is that it should be a practical guide, an informative companion during the pressured, lonely, and at times bewildering and frightening process of bringing a film into the world—a process that can be among the most precious achievements of anyone's life.

1
How Might Zen Relate to the Director?

In what ways might the layman who happens to be a filmmaker, or perhaps any layman, understand the meaning of Zen? And then, even if they understand it to some extent, how might an ancient, esoteric practice connect with the task of the film director, an activity that has come into being relatively recently? Given a basic grasp of the venerable practice of Zen, might a director find relevance in it to their self and their work? Could there be connections that are more than fanciful?

Let's first consider what we might understand as some central precepts of Zen.

1. Living in the moment, in the present
2. Living openly, with *what is*
3. Letting go of one's self, of one's identity
4. Letting go of one's knowledge
5. An emptiness for open and clear seeing
6. Sitting still and being
7. Zen is presence, Zen is you, you and Zen are one
8. Engaging with the universe
9. Connecting with deep consciousness
10. Zen-channeling as crafting the power of life

1. Living in the moment, in the present

Although the director has to keep multiple considerations in their head—everything that constitutes the big picture of their creative formulation and the practical and logistical complexity of a production—they need also to focus on what is happening, or needs to happen, at any given moment.

The director cannot afford to miss a trick, even if this might seem barely possible given all they have to remember, have to keep in the back of their mind, have to be constantly prioritizing, and all that might be unfolding around them, much of it of no immediate— or indeed any—concern to them.

During the formulation, through the endless meetings and deep collaboration with the creative team; while location scouting; amid the shoot, with its pressured schedule and the panoply of equipment, personnel, and activity that surrounds and enables it; and later, through the edit—from assembly to final cut, sound work, and the final honing of the image, right up to the previews—the director must maintain a keen awareness of the moment.

If they do not, whatever passes in that instant of inattention may later return to haunt them.

This aspect of Zen, then, seems especially pertinent to the director. What stands in tension with it, however, is the filmmaker's need to retain that immense reservoir of unresolved issues, challenges to be met, and priorities to be decided—matters the director cannot, and should not, ignore or forget.

The paradox here—and there are many in a director's work—is that this state of living in the moment is itself informed and sustained by an awareness of the film's connective tissue, developed over the preceding weeks and months of the filmmaker's engagement with the project, as well as by their intentions for what lies ahead.

The duration of the making of the film illuminates the moment, but the moment itself demands recognition and agency in the director's process.

2. Living openly, with *what is*

Related to that first aspect of Zen is the need for a director not to shield their self from the reality of the circumstances of their filmmaking. An acceptance and embrace of what actually *is*—perhaps in terms of budget, in the restrictions of a location, in the constraints of the shooting schedule, in available resources—and then the bringing to bear of practical and creative inventiveness to get the best of what might be available, forms an essential skill of the director.

One designed image can say more than the expansive vista of a high-budget studio movie. A dozen extras judiciously placed and moving in coordination with the camera and the frame can be more effective than a hundred configured arbitrarily. A camera angle chosen with emotional impact on the viewer or "critical" comment on subject matter in mind can avoid the need to show everything when that cannot be afforded or set up without wasting valuable hours of shooting.

Restriction, limitation, and challenge are part and parcel of the creative process.

The director who could have everything they want for as long as they want it—if that were ever possible—would in all probability find their process lost. For the functioning director, what *is* offers the conduit to what *can be*.

3. Letting go of one's self, of one's identity

In the face of the challenges of making a movie true to itself, one that takes on a life above and beyond that of its director, ego can prove the worst of saboteurs. The director's specific persona, cultural assumptions, and elements of fixed mindset, if not tempered by the aware filmmaker, can further limit the creative oxygen their movie needs as it comes together.

Even in an auto-fictional film in which a protagonist may serve as a proxy for the writer-director, the fiction must find its own life, independent of the personal history on which it is founded. This imperative applies equally to works of fantasy, for the director—as we will see in later chapters—is at once explorer and follower, commander and servicer. At certain points in the making of a film, the director's intention increasingly comes face to face with the film's own needs, which may not be the same. When this occurs, the filmmaker must be willing to let go of preconceptions—and even of aspects of their own identity—in order to allow the identity of the film itself to take precedence.

There are instances, however, in which the director's identity—rooted in background and community—may be central to their material and to the making of their film. Even then, an identity connected to something larger than the filmmaker's individual self—often a terrain of its own breadth and contradiction—may need to take precedence if the director is to fully realize their process, rising above personal concerns and private agendas.

4. Letting go of one's knowledge

This aspect of Zen might seem contradictory to the work of the director who has perhaps honed their skills over years of experience, learning from previous failures and successes as they come to make each film.

A director who fails to learn from experience and who omits to bring the wisdom thus accrued into their work would surely be doomed to starting from square one with every film they come to make. Looking at this aspect of Zen from a different angle, however, no director could learn from their experiences if they were not open to new insights.

When the director finds something is not working, even if it may have worked in the past, there might be some element in the present situation that doesn't correlate with previous scenarios, something that might be rectified. If it cannot, the filmmaker must cast aside preconceptions and think afresh.

Moreover, contributions, tough questions, and challenges from the cast and creative team may not always be adequately met by the director's current resources of craft. When this happens, such encounters can serve as a spur to discovering and embracing new approaches.

Should past experience result in a fixed mindset, should previous inventiveness end up as present dogma, dysfunction will inevitably follow. When the director is unafraid to let go of such barriers, they discover within themselves the resources to meet new challenges, to come to terms with them, and to continue growing as a filmmaker.

5. An emptiness for open and clear seeing
Alfred Hitchcock said:

I know we're only human. We do go in for these various emotions—call them negative emotions. But when all these are removed and you can look forward and the road is clear ahead, and now you're going to create something—I think that's as happy as I'll ever want to be.

Reflecting on these insights from the master, we can see what the director might desire in the best of all worlds, as opposed to what they actually face. If this aspect of Zen is one the director will find elusive, it is also one they must in some way facilitate.

With so much that the filmmaker must attend to — creative challenges, practical problems, political dynamics, emotional tensions, crew intrigues, the personal agendas of others — they need to be able to compartmentalize issues and intentions in order to find the space for the emptiness essential to "open and clear seeing."

That, given the pressures of the schedule and often unanticipated circumstances, isn't easy. With recognition of this Zen fundamental, though, the director at least knows what they have to find — elusive as that may prove.

6. Sitting still and being

How could such a rarefied aspiration relate in any way to the animated, energetic, and restless director? They may indeed sit still at times, while formulating their film, or hunkered down watching the actors on a monitor, or working with the editor through the stages of post. But they will find precious few moments for simply *being*.

All the more essential that they set aside times to be alone, to empty their mind (by whatever means that work for them), and to appreciate this sense of simply *being*. Neither active nor passive, this state of being is at the center of all else.

Were there no being, there would be no director, no story-making, no filmmaking, no film.

Perhaps this aspect of Zen is not so incompatible with the task of directing, but is, in fact, obligatory.

7. Zen as presence, Zen as you, you and Zen are one

In considering Bresson's notion of directing one's self, this element of Zen philosophy would seem central to our understanding. Whatever it is that directs one's self—and especially before one's self directs someone else—it has to have greater compass and less limitation than that of the self. Allowing for that agency—recognizing it as a "you" beyond yourself, according to the practice of Zen—enables a unity of being.

If this sounds insufficiently hard-headed for the working director in the hectic and pressured environment of filmmaking, a world in which the graph of stress ascends steeply as budget and size of production rise, the apparent incongruity is all the more reason for its relevance.

The production, the schedule, the crew, and the equipment are the means by which a film gets made. The director, material, humanity, and universe are the domains of creative filmmaking. Whatever the daily activity of production, the filmmaker, while recognizing this, needs to be free of its encumbrances and distractions.

It seems to me that this—the filmmaker's "presence," their unity—is what a basic grasp of Zen can offer the director.

8. Engaging with the universe

In Chapter Three, "Voices the Director Hears," I discuss what I call "the voice of the universe." This may suggest a kind of nebulous cosmic "vibe"—something some of us have felt, but which to the grounded practitioner might seem rather flighty. Yet if it does, it also includes the simple, coincidental sights, events, and people the director comes across during the filmmaking process.

The director, their antennae adequately attuned, finds their self in a position to recognize the sundry signs and signals this "universe" offers, as seemingly unrelated incidents and remarks can spark new insights into their material and process.

9. Connecting with deep consciousness

Paradox! The universe, deep consciousness. And yet... both are the domains of the creative soul. Together, they eclipse the narrowness and self-interest of the ego.

In Chapters Four, Five, and Six, we will explore the conscious and the subconscious self and how the filmmaker might reflect on ways to assess and connect with them.

10. Zen-channeling as crafting the power of life

Might this rather daunting observation be related to Bresson's apothegm? Isn't he suggesting a "channeling" (a key term, it seems to me) when he writes of directing one's self? Doesn't a movie require "the power of life"—in its creators, in itself? Isn't the notion of "crafting" essential to the filmmaker?

With these seminal aspects of Zen in mind, we can now move on to the next element of this book's title: the director.

2
What Do We Mean by "The Director"?

*To be a film director, you need three things:
energy, curiosity, and patience.*

Agnieszka Holland

The British actor Bob Hoskins, after directing a feature, described his experience as *like being pecked to death by sparrows*. Many directors would surely agree. The unremitting stream of questions, demands, unexpected eventualities, and seemingly insuperable problems and crises can render the position of "director" one that few, were they aware of what it actually entails, would choose to take up.

The great John Ford, on the other hand, with typical unassuming frankness, said that *directing is a job of work*.

That's as may be, but what a job it is! Even Ford had to deal with studios who didn't give directors final cut or even a seat in the cutting room. To circumvent this egregious intrusion on his vision, Ford would cover the lens with his hand until the moment he called "Action!," and then again the instant he called "Cut!" As a result, the film could only be edited the way he intended. Some "job" indeed!—to foresee every cut, every rhythm and surge of energy, every shot size and angle on the screen, without a shred of flexibility left for adjustment in the edit.

Ford also had to contend with that other challenge: working with movie star John Wayne. Anecdote has it that, though Wayne may have become Ford's fictional alter ego, the director's respect for him was far from unconditional. Yet their collaboration yielded some of cinema's most iconic performances—testament to Ford's intuition, artistry, and unerring skill in handling people.

How, then, might we describe the director? Here are some of the possibilities.

1. Artist
2. Craftsperson
3. Leader
4. Diplomat
5. Politician
6. Persuader
7. Listener
8. Challenger
9. Collaborator
10. Explorer
11. Investigator/Detective
12. Navigator/Pilot
13. Connector
14. Parent
15. Teacher
16. Student
17. Loner

Let's consider each of these categories in turn.

1. Artist

A term many would rather avoid. The implications of the word, for those who see themselves as more hard-headed, might include the indulgent prioritizing of self-expression over functional practice, of vulnerable sensitivity above the resilience essential to the film-maker in the grip of logistical and budgetary constraints, the pressure of time, and domineering producers and executives—quite apart from the multiple challenges of making a movie that's any good, or even simply of making a movie.

For some, the word might suggest a focus on individual, inner process rather than engagement with the imperatives of the material, with telling the story, with cast and crew, and with "the suits."

They might feel it implies a lack of budgetary responsibility or a suspicion that personal agendas might come between director and movie, that the "artistic director" might impose their obsessions and hang-ups on the film to its detriment.

Yet directors who would shoot and cut a scene in exactly the same way as each other are unlikely to be the best (perhaps not even adequate) filmmakers. There must be a connection between the director and their experience of life—their worldview, social and cultural background, and psyche—and what they choose or agree to direct, if the result is to be anything more than work performed by rote. Even if Zen-aware directors let go of their identity, these differences will not be eradicated.

Some, even notable filmmakers, dismiss the notion of "creative vision" as a nebulous affectation. But the singular revelation of the human condition that can be achieved in filmmaking (and often by those who may not realize it's in their work) is no affectation. Nor can innovative cinematic language that serves the movie be merely cosmetic. On the contrary, it must represent the true unity of content and style, so that substance *is* style and style substance. Such organic unity renders a film a work of art.

We should acknowledge, though, that directors may feel the role of artist as a burden of responsibility they could do without. To direct a film that coheres at all is daunting enough. So long as there is no cynicism, no resentment toward the filmmaking process and its personnel, and there is pride in one's work, this work-manlike mindset, as well as that of the artist, does not preclude consideration and indeed incorporation of what I'm calling the Zen of the Director.

2. Craftsperson

Most would find this term more down-to-earth. Ford's "job of work" involves the *crafting* of the film through the application of several inter-functional skills, each serving the task of storytelling and its engagement with the viewer. The formulation of approach in all areas, the visualization of the narrative, the eliciting of performances, the staging, shooting, cutting, employ-ment of sound and music, the modulation of emotion and tone—each constitutes an exacting task.

No director, no matter how anti-formalist or avowedly spontaneous, can avoid the utilization of craft in making a movie.

An informed sense of craft, a continuing explora-tion of its principles, complexities, and agile applica-tion offers the director a breadth of perspective on their work that the director's Zen can serve well.

3. Leader

Few directors would deny seeing themselves as leaders. If they are not guiding the exploration, articulation, and realization of a film, it can scarcely be said they are directing it. Some exercise tighter control than others. Michelangelo Antonioni and John Cassavetes, for instance, were polar opposites: the former orchestrating every granular detail of gesture, movement, and frame; the latter cultivating an illusion of spontaneity in performance and mise-en-scène that would become the envy of those he inspired.

There are, of course, many kinds of directors, from the tyrant at one extreme to the enabler of everyone at the other, not to mention some who hide behind the abilities of their team or are deliberately self-effacing, exerting a more or less invisible stewardship. Across the spectrum, however, most of them, in their own way, must be in charge.

The loneliness of this responsibility, and the vulnerability that goes with it, can be terrifying for most of us. But it is also seductive. Power going to a director's head leaves little room for any checks and balances of the self. It tends also to alienate one's collaborators.

For both the insecure leader and their dictatorial alter ego, an introduction to the Zen of the Director may foster more effective leadership. This concept— best understood as a resource—can offer insight into the ways ego undermines the capacity to lead.

4. Diplomat

The director, whose authority may not always be respected, must at times act as a diplomat. This can prove especially trying for the filmmaker whose intentions are repeatedly misunderstood, ignored, or obstructed, yet who must persist in pursuing their objectives. Diplomatic skills are therefore invaluable amid the daily negotiations inevitable in any collaborative art or business.

5. Politician

The director must also possess the guile of a politician. Yet when politics enters the filmmaking process—as it almost inevitably will—there arises the danger that the director may cease to be truthful to either themselves or their film. The Zen of the Director can offer guidance in navigating interactions shaped by politics and guarding against the dangers inherent in the politician's role: self-serving manipulation and the urge to control.

6. Persuader

Guile, empathy, patience, clarity, respect, listening—all are virtues of the persuasive Zen director as they interact with their team to achieve their intentions.

7. Listener

When the director listens—to their team, their actors, and their own inner interlocutors—they open themselves to insights, understandings, and approaches they might never have discovered on their own.

Listening is an aspect of a director's "people skills." When members of the team know the director is listening to them, when they know their opinions are valued, they are more likely to invest their full commitment than if they feel ignored or disrespected. Ultimately, of course, it's the director and the film that will benefit from this.

When the director attunes their antennae to that ineffable thing, the "universe," ideas can come, seemingly, out of nowhere. Inspiration tends to have a bad name, but if it is precluded by Ford's "job of work," its unexplainable instances cannot be denied by those who experience it. When we say an idea "strikes us," we acknowledge this. It is as if something—the universe—has given that idea agency.

Listening, without and within, is central to the Zen of the Director.

8. Collaborator

Even the hyphenate writer, cinematographer, editor, composer-director must collaborate with someone or other along the line. There are few, if any, directors who do not at some point benefit from productive collaboration with others. There is considerable skill involved in interactions of this kind, for it is the director—who possesses both the keenest sense of a film's connective tissue and the clearest vision of it—who must ultimately orchestrate and guide these exchanges.

Equally important is the collaboration the director has with their self, and the listening and challenging it entails. Self-collaboration is very much the central facet of Bresson's "directing one's self."

The Zen of the Director will be of considerable value here, encompassing the director's collaboration with their team and with their writer, their cast, and their own self.

9. Challenger

There can be no collaboration without challenges. Effective collaboration does not arise among people who agree on everything. It is the differences of opinion and perspective—the to-and-fro of ideas—that lead to the kind of decision-making that makes collaboration truly effective. And, of course, the director needs to challenge their own self and the obstacles this presents—an essential aspect of their director's Zen.

10. Explorer

The director does not know everything. Not about their art, their craft, not about the movie they are currently making, not about their self, not about life.

The director's task is to discover what the film is, and what it requires. They explore the territory of their movie, its narrative, tone, style, its visual language, its auditory language, its casting.

The director is a pioneer, the pioneer of the film world and characters.

The effective director is not a reductivist, not an "it all boils down to this" adherent, no cynic who has seen it all before. Their work is not a fait accompli before they actually begin. They know there will be new challenges requiring fresh approaches.

An explorer in an unknown land will inevitably take certain risks. If the director, as explorer, is also willing to take risks, these may yield unexpected gifts and lead to unanticipated connections. If there are no risks, no dangers, if the filming process is entirely safe (in a creative sense), there will be no gifts.

The threat of failure can be debilitating, yet without it there can be no discovery.

For the director, a sense of their Zen can make the prospect of a wrong risk less frightening.

And let's remember: an error can contain the seed of progress.

11. Investigator
It can also be useful for the director to think of their self as an investigator, or detective, as they explore the nature of their material and its connective tissue, and as they research and ascertain the possible means — artistically, technically, and logistically — of achieving the intention of their film. This is also an integral aspect of the collaborative and challenging elements of their process.

Through the Zen of the Director, the filmmaker may also investigate what thoughts may be hidden at the back of their mind, hints or hunches that have not yet been acknowledged or recognized and potential defense mechanisms that prevent them from finding optimal ways forward.

12. Navigator/Pilot

If the explorer ventures into unknown territory, the navigator, or marine pilot, works from maps and charts to ensure the route taken avoids unnecessary dangers and unwanted diversions and leads to the desired destination. This perspective may seem incompatible with the notion of the director as explorer, but while the director is far from all-seeing, they are unlikely to be entirely blind. Although they may not have a clear map, they surely have some foreknowledge of what their task entails.

They can draw from previous experience, from their knowledge of cinema and filmmaking and its production processes, from the nature and voice of their material, and, with a basic understanding of Zen, from their sense of their self in order to take their bearings.

With this awareness, they can then pilot the ship of creative filmmaking, and of the production that serves it.

13. Connector

The director has the task of "connecting" in the following spheres:

A. They find and build the connective tissue of their material

i) within the narrative;
ii) within the visual language;
iii) within the soundscape;
iv) across visual and auditory languages;
v) across the narrative and its telling through image
     and sound;
vi) and across actors and camera.

B. They connect the creative team and their crafts to each other, and to the material.

C. They connect the film to the audience.

D. They connect the elements of their self, in order to function effectively.

The Zen of the Director is vital to all of these categories. Central is the connection of the self without the barrier of ego—although directors, like any artist, must also recognize and utilize contradictory and indeed turbulent aspects within their psyches. Indeed, it is those very conflicts that nourish drama and story. The purpose of connecting with such conflicts is not to nullify their power but to acknowledge, embrace, and bring to bear their irreconcilable energies on the director's engagement with their material.

14. Parent

As with leaders, there are good parents and bad, and others who are merely indifferent. In any production, team, crew, and above all actors may regard the director as a kind of parent figure, though few directors welcome—or have time for—the role. If this deference is met with respect, then that, ideally, can become mutual.

It is surely also incumbent on the director, especially in their relationship with the actor, to be protective of them. There is a dichotomy here, of course. The director must challenge the actors to give their best, a task that can prove bracing, even emotionally precarious, and in the worst instances might cross the line into abuse. This can also apply to the creative and production teams.

Precarity—the acceptance, and even the embrace, of the danger of failure, perhaps even the fear that a project may prove worthless—should form at least one aspect of any artistic pursuit, even if it renders directors far from perfect "parents." Collaboration modifies this role too, in that the actor can offer possibilities the director hasn't considered, and production designers, costume designers, cinematographers, and editors can bring fresh approaches and solutions of which the director may not have been aware.

A sense of the director's Zen facilitates these interactions. It may also enable the director to become a parent to their own self (directing their self) and to guide their self as they guide others.

15. Teacher

Although some entirely capable directors fall short when teaching a class of students, many cannot help but be teachers to their team. This function (related to that of parent) arises when the director articulates questions and challenges posed by the film, exploring possibilities and criteria for finding the best way forward. In this context, some will be educators—not only within the confines of the film being made, but also in broader concerns and concepts of filmmaking, and cinema in general, which others may take with them on completion of the film.

Whether or not a director is also a teacher, and even if formally trained, they must be capable of learning: from their mistakes, from what works and what doesn't, from the cast, from the creative team, and from the work of other filmmakers.

The twin activities of education and self-education form a central aspect of the Zen of the Director.

16. Student

This is an important function of the director. They are the student of their cast, of their crew, and above all of their film. Their directing Zen is their classroom, its discourse, challenges, questions, solutions, and realization.

A good student sets out to learn. A good student inspires their peers to learn. To make a movie is to learn to make a movie. To learn to make a movie is to make it.

17. Loner

Unlike the novelist, the director works with many collaborators throughout the processes of production and creation. But, like the novelist, the director—if they are not merely working by rule and rote—must form, articulate, and execute the story and storytelling, along with all the multifunctional elements involved. The responsibility for the creative success of the film is ultimately theirs. They will also be held accountable for the commercial success of movies with any substantial —perhaps even any—budget.

The director's position is a lonely one.

The "loner," however, is someone who thrives on their solitude. That there should be any measure of solitude in a collaborative and frequently sociable—and on occasion, unfortunately, combative—environment, seems a paradox. But the Zen of the Director provides for an embrace of paradox: the director is an interactive loner, a collaborative leader, a listening communicator, a teaching student and a being of many more seemingly incompatible qualities.

This is the beauty of the vocation.

3
Voices the Director Hears

The point is not to direct someone, but to direct one's self.

Let's consider the implications. Bresson seems to be saying that in the process of directing one's self, directing the *inner*, one will find one's self directing the *outer*, that without directing their self, the director cannot truly be directing anyone else.

We might think of the wisdom in this apothegm as lying at the heart of what I call The Zen of the Director. It is the wellspring—the source of nourishment and of substance.

But how can one direct one's self?

Who or what is it that does that directing?

What is this self and what are the elements that are being directed?

How does this relate to directing "someone" else?

Let's consider what precisely it might that is directing one's self, if not the self itself.

To begin, we take the notion of *the voice*: the internal interlocutor, or interlocutors we hear—or many of us hear—as we weigh how to solve a problem, choose between alternatives, or entertain a new idea or possibility.

These are "speakers" with whom the filmmaker might have a dialogue or whom they might at times prefer to brush aside. In triangulating the director-material relationship, these interlopers, placed between the director and their film, the director and their world, can be helpful or not, can be enabling or destructive, depending on natures that seem ever protean.

When the director steps outside the self—so far as they are able—to observe the nature of those inner voices and the influence they exert on thought and decision-making, and when they learn to temper that influence (again, as far as they can), they are already engaged in directing the self. There follow the external voices: most important among them the voice of the material, a voice that speaks to the self and to which the director should listen not only for what it has to say but also for how their self receives and reacts to it. Is their response functional, or skewed by some internal agenda? Is it drawing on a connection the director finds, or on some resonance, either sympathetic or uncomfortable? Or is it defensively building obstacles to understanding? In which case the director might need to readjust their engagement with that material.

The director would be wise to also recognize and value the external voices of the creative team, perhaps of the crew, and indeed of anyone connected with a production—or perhaps not connected at all! How does the self react to these voices? How successfully does it assess the value of these messages? Is the self making the best use of the insights offered? Could it be *over-* or *under*valuing a message, perhaps for personal or political reasons?

These voices come in a variety of forms, inner and outer.

Inner
1. The whisperer
2. The saboteur
3. The bully
4. The superego
5. The doubter
6. The troublemaker
7. The voice of impulse
8. The voice of intuition
9. The iconoclast
10. The subversive
11. The mischief-maker
12. The practitioner
13. The not-knower
14. The questioner

Outer
1. The universe
2. The "voice of the angel"
3. The connections
4. The material
5. The collaborator
6. The cynic
7. The mentor

Inner
1. The whisperer
On the one hand, this insidious inner voice may sow doubt, its sibilant nagging creating a sense of unease. The whisperer may seek to unnerve, its quiet insistence eating away at the director's search for steady decision-making, even at their confidence.

On the other hand, the whisperer might be a kindly advisor, whose gentle intervention allows the

filmmaker time to consider matters that, given immediate pressure, might prompt a poor decision.

It is this ambiguity that renders the whisperer a
challenging voice to interpret.

2. The saboteur

More direct than the whisperer, the inner saboteur
offers the director a perverse agency in pressured situations: the agency to bring their house crashing down.
The saboteur offers safety in failure. Of all the adversaries within, it is among the most corrosive, providing
the self-destructive comfort of disempowering not
only the others, but, crucially, the filmmaker themself.
The director must at all times be on their guard against
the saboteur.

3. The bully

Worse than the saboteur, the bully of the self acts out
of spite, offering the director not only the consola-
tion of failure but worse: the pain of self-humiliation.
Like physical and emotional bullies, it prompts shame
and dysfunction. Additionally, the bully's voice may
prompt the director in turn to bully their cast and
crew.

4. The superego

This holier-than-thou puritan denies something essential to both the artist and the functioning director: the
contradictory dimensions of humanity. It demands
"good behavior," urging the filmmaker to conform, to
follow the rules—the diktats of some manual to which
they have perhaps sworn obeisance. The superego
insists that respectability, not respect, and popular
approval should be the filmmaker's aim.

5. The doubter

This voice can be incapacitating, but might also serve as a useful check on impulsive or self-serving decision-making. If it renders the director constantly unsure, it can be debilitating. Yet the filmmaker without the capacity to doubt can have no robust belief in their process.

Just as there can be no faith without doubt, so the acceptance of healthy doubt is integral to the Zen of the Director. Yet the corrosive agency of unhealthy doubt must be guarded against. The director's Zen—with its practice of patient, open reflection—can help discern one from the other.

6. The troublemaker

A combination of the aforementioned voices, it is hard to know when to trust this internal, shape-shifting interlocutor. The maker of good trouble is worth listening to, but the maker of bad trouble is just a mask for the saboteur. Awareness of the Zen of the Director can assist the filmmaker in distinguishing one from the other.

7. The voice of impulse

Impulse makes life easier. No need for doubt, no need even for thought, when impulse is acted upon. When, however, it is not, when the director considers it first, the value of impulse as a facet of intuition, an aspect of the *voice of the gut*, can become central to the director's creative process.

This instinctive, often visceral interlocutor has much to contribute to the Zen of the Director when valued—though not so much when blindly followed.

8. The voice of intuition

Connected to the voice of impulse but quieter and more assured, the voice of intuition constitutes a deep foundation of the Zen of the Director. A filmmaker without intuition is doomed to obey the strictures of rule and rote. With intuition, they have a sense of the nature of all other voices and the degree of authenticity of their creative processes and decision-making.

9. The iconoclast

When intuition meets common assumption, the iconoclast emerges. Groupthink, whether within the filmmaker's process, the narrative and cinematic dimensions of the material, or the formulation of their visual and auditory address to the viewer, will result in indifferent filmmaking. The Zen of the Director is not a concept of passivity but of agile facilitation. The iconoclast is an active and unflinching facet of this Zen.

10. The subversive

Similar to the iconoclast, the subversive seeks to upend presupposed notions—especially of a cultural and moral nature—too readily accepted by many filmmakers, by insufficiently developed material, and often by audiences.

Pandering to these assumptions and playing safe in order to gain the approval of viewers all too happy to congratulate themselves on their righteousness denudes stories of human truth and soul. Simply accepting unthinking, conventional, or modish approaches to filmmaking similarly handicaps the director.

Safety does not lie in conformism—but, then, the artist can never be safe. The Zen of the Director offers not a place of safety but of being, a field fertile for both the practical and creative aspects of the filmmaker's work.

11. The mischief-maker

Incorporating the voices of the iconoclast and the subversive, the mischief-maker takes delight in upsetting the apple cart. The mischief to be made, however, is not mere disruption for its own sake but creative innovation that, while it can be hugely enjoyable, defying expectations of the film and its audience, *has to work*, has to connect with other elements of the narrative and the storytelling. What is fun has function, too, in the director's Zen.

12. The practitioner

Apparently the antithesis of several of the previous voices, the practitioner is the voice of craft and experience, a problem-solver who makes best use of circumstance and of budgetary and other limitations encountered in the course of production. A filmmaker has to incorporate practicality into their artistic process—and the two are far from incompatible. Indeed, the challenge of limitation may prompt the director to examine more closely the purpose and intention of an aspect of the narrative, its imagery, and their implications for their storytelling.

With their Zen, the director's head is not lost in the clouds but more closely engaged with their material and their task. They are present. An essential aspect of their engagement lies in the filmmaker's adept practicality both in the moment and throughout the making of the film.

13. The not-knower

The director who thinks they know everything is in no position to work practically or inventively. Their claimed omniscience is a form of cynicism, a shutting down of the directorial process. The all-knowing director may think they work from experience but they forget their discoveries along the way, unless they never discovered anything but simply and obediently took from rule and rote without thinking for themselves. In such a case, their knowing is a manifestation of a defensiveness which obstructs their filmmaking.

The not-knowing voice is by contrast well placed to embark and follow through the voyage of discovery that making a movie presents, allowing the director to learn from their material, their art, their team, their process, and from their film itself as it comes together.

The director aware of their not-knowing voice is quite different from the ignorant director. The voice of the not-knower is, paradoxically, an integral element of the insight afforded by the Zen of the Director.

14. The questioner

Enabled by the not-knower, more neutral than the subversive or the mischief-maker, the questioner stimulates the exploration of the director's material, their filmmaking, and its address to the viewer. Taking nothing for granted, the questioner brings in an objective perspective outside of the director's own sensibility. Through a lack of any agenda, the questioner allows the director's material to speak for itself.

This voice connects closely with the selflessness that—together with an acknowledgement and awareness of the self—provides a foundation for the Zen of the Director.

Outer
1. The universe

This is an ongoing gift to the director. Sights, events, moments in the filmmaker's everyday life can somehow connect with, and offer insight into, a film's needs, its challenges, and to the solutions that may be hidden in its connective tissue.

Someone among the crew, the cast, in production or on its peripheries may say something that proves invaluable if the director has their antennae attuned to such overheard messages. If this "universe" sounds like fanciful metaphysics, it is actually a resource requiring minimal effort on the part of the director, so long as, together with a focus in their material, they are keeping their eyes and ears open.

While the Zen of the Director incorporates the director's solitude, the concept also embraces the notion of the filmmaker as part of their community and world, and these, in turn, as parts of the universe.

2. The "voice of the angel"

In his novel *Kepler*, about the 16th/17th-century astronomer, John Banville writes:

When the solution came, it came, as always, through the back door of the mind, hesitating shyly, an announcing angel dazed by the immensity of its journey.

In a culture enamored of the "work ethic" (although work and ethics are unrelated), the notion that solutions to a problem, that insight itself, might arrive without effort on the part of the receiver, would seem heretical. Inspiration has a bad name. Perspiration is understood as the key to effective process. And yet it is in moments of repose, of walking, showering, simply making a cup of coffee or performing some menial task unrelated to the filmmaker's work that some of the most profound realizations can arise. The filmmaker who remains forever immersed in their task to the exclusion of all else allows no opportunity for this voice.

Another novelist, V. S. Pritchett, wrote of *the determined stupor out of which greater novelists work*. The imperative here is the *need* for the fallow moments in which this voice might speak to the artist, and its consequent absence when work and its so-called "ethic" shut it out.

Like the voice of the universe, the "voice of the angel" is a free gift. With their Zen of the Director, the filmmaker is open to such sudden illumination.

Perhaps one might better understand this as an interior voice? In her book *Plotting and Writing Suspense Fiction*, Patricia Highsmith writes of the notebook she would keep by the side of her bed in which she would jot down her middle-of-the-night thoughts that she wouldn't otherwise necessarily recall the following day.

Such insights from the deep subconscious might be equated with "the voice of the angel," except that they emerge from the sleeping mind rather than sundry activities or moments of rest during the day.

See Chapter Six for further consideration of how the filmmaker might acknowledge and address their subconscious self.

3. The connections
Were the filmmaker to do no work at all, or to fail to commit comprehensively to the demands of their creative and practical process through their connection to it, the "voice of the angel," and, indeed, every other voice, would surely fail to speak up.

The voice of connection may come painfully slowly, struggling to get through and unable to do so without constant work. Not a matter of any "ethic," this is more an aspect of *function*. As the director—like the writer—persists with an ever-deepening engagement with their film, as they make progress with and develop greater understanding of the multiple elements of narrative, its storytelling, and of the practical challenges of making their movie, so their growing sense of the connective tissue of their film brings out its evolving unity.

The voice of connection grows stronger through formulation, shooting, and editing, as one element increasingly speaks to another. By focusing on the journey of their process rather than its destination—which they cannot fully know, and which, if they think they do, may constrain the voice of their material—the director is best placed to uncover the steps in the evolution of their own understanding.

The patience the director requires in order for this voice to be heard most clearly is a fundamental aspect of the Zen of the Director. If we might step aside from Zen to Tao for a moment, these words from Lao Tzu offer an invaluable perspective on this voice:

A good traveler has no fixed plans, and is not intent on arriving.

A good director is such a traveler. Even while they know perfectly well that they are responsible for bringing in a successful film, they are not attached to outcome. As the director connects one element of their material and its realization to another, they find they are focusing on their journey, yet in doing so come closer to its destination. This contradiction is a fundamental aspect of the Zen of the Director.

4. The material
Going hand in hand with the voice of connection is the voice of the director's material itself. The filmmaker's process is something of a paradox. In one respect the director formulates intention in all aspects of their art, which they apply to their material. In another, their

material tells them what it is and what it needs in order to become that.

Although some directors may be wary of the term "creative vision," which the pragmatic aspect of their craft may leave them to regard as too nebulous to be of any value, they will nevertheless (and quite rightly) hold in their mind a preconception of the film they wish to bring to the screen.

At the same time there is an element of their activity that works in the opposite direction. As a movie increasingly comes together, so it speaks to the director with greater clarity and insistence on what it needs to be. Its messages prompt the filmmaker not so much to betray their original intentions as enable them to *realize* more closely the *authentic* nature of their film.

Such is the creative agility demanded of the director. The fixed mindset has no place in their approach. Symbiosis of one form or another is central to the Zen of the Director by which the vectors of intention and discovery constitute a foundational dynamic of film-making's evolutionary nature.

What, though, are the registers of the address the material makes to its director?

There are two fundamental aspects: the small picture and the big picture—the granular and the architectural. By switching from consideration of one to the other, small to big, big to small, by allowing one to inform the other throughout the film's evolution—from initial idea to story to screenplay to formulation to the shoot, through editing to the final stages of post-production—the director enables their self to hear the voice of their material most effectively and to benefit from it to the full.

It is essential also for the director to consider the voice of their material when they are confronted by logistical or budgetary challenges. What may present itself as a practical problem may, with the intervention of the material's true needs, reveal a creative solution the director might otherwise not have discovered. Instead of reacting with a compromise, the director may find that revision and simplification can lead to a deepening of their approach.

5. The collaborator
In harmony with the voice of the material is the voice of the collaborator, offering fresh insights and solutions the director alone might not have come up with. Production designer, costume designer, cinematographer, editor, producer, cast—all have voices. The director should listen to them whether they agree or not. The Zen of the Director is not about self-fortification but an equipoise of practical and creative minds, and of interaction both within and without.

6. The cynic
This external voice, from those who seek reductive, world-weary disdain for the process and for other people, is utterly destructive and has no place in The Zen of the Director. "Actors are cattle" (which Hitchcock did not say*), or "It's a business—art has nothing to do with it," or any similar advice, borne of cynicism, bitterness, or nihilism, serves only to satisfy the insatiable negativity of those who wish to shut the filmmaker down.

7. The mentor
Many directors, perhaps most, will have benefited from the mentorship of one or more particular persons at some point in their development. A parent or grand-

---

* Though Hitchcock did apparently say that actors should be "treated like cattle."

parent, aunt or uncle, someone acting in one of those capacities, a teacher or professor, a filmmaker with whom they have served some form of apprenticeship, even someone who may not have even realized the effect they were having, will often provide a lasting voice in the head of the filmmaker. The director will hear in their mind their familiar voice as they go about taking the decisions required to make their film. In that sense, this might be considered an inner voice.

The imagined guiding voice of the true mentor, although in life they may be unavailable offers the filmmaker an invaluable and ongoing interlocution.

With the Zen of the Director, the filmmaker recognizes authentic mentors and brings their experience, insights, and philosophy into their creative process.

With a sense of the voices the director might hear, we can now consider the nature of the "one's self"—as Bresson puts it—that the director directs.

4
The Director and the Self

Thought:

The director's self should not get in the way of the material.

Response:

Ignore it, deny it, fail to recognize it, and that's exactly what it will do.

Self-awareness, or awareness of the self, can make an invaluable contribution to the navigation of the filmmaking process, just as it does in the navigation of life. No matter how much we try, however, we can never be completely schematic in our understanding of ourselves. Rather than this presenting a problem, though, it's all to the good.

When the Brazilian novelist Clarice Lispector commented *I want to be a mystery to myself*, she reminded us that both in the artist and in their art, there needs to be mystery. This is true for the filmmaker, although if this were all there were to their approach and there were nothing else, it would be hard for them to direct their self, to have their voices and what would be a completely mysterious self interact.

Let us look at the elements that might constitute the director's self. Here are some adjectives and descriptions that point to such aspects:

Intuitive, practical, emotional, visceral, neural, enteric, intellectual. (Forget the "overthinking" canard. The problem we face most often is rather *under-*thinking, or not thinking at all.)

And some others:

Mischievous, inventive, naive, experienced, practiced, with more to learn, visionary, questioning, exploring, selfless, selfish, shadow, childlike.

Let's reflect on these multiple facets.

The intuitive and practical self would seem contradictory, yet both are essential to the effective director who, given the vicissitudes, eventualities, and accidents concomitant with making any movie, cannot rely solely on their creative self to fashion absolutely the storytelling of their film in the way a novelist might control the nature of their novel.

The director's process incorporates the challenges of logistical and budgetary realities, of the strengths and weaknesses of their selves and the creative team, of casting availabilities, of the actors' abilities, of the pressure of schedule and time, and of unanticipated problems. In the face of these, a director's practicality is an essential resource.

Intuition and instinct, on the other hand, are indispensable to any but the most uninspired filmmaker. The student will not become a successful director by simply digesting received wisdom from "how to" courses in directing and from the platitudes they peddle.

There is no complete class in directing because intuition and instinct cannot be taught. Unlike the filmmaker's practical abilities, they come from the subconscious self (that we will consider later).

Similarly, the emotional, visceral, neural, enteric aspects of the self derive from the subconscious and from our raw physicality, while the intellectual facility tends to be more the product of the conscious self.

Many artists, business people, and filmmaking educators are quick to criticize the intellect. Seen as pertaining to theory rather than practice, intellect is mistaken for esoteric academism rather than the precious human resource that it is. Seen as the enemy of both intuition and practice, it is regarded by many educators and practitioners as a false engagement with the world when in truth it is the engine of inquiry and the rigorous consideration of the director's material along with the address to the viewer the director formulates.

Indeed, as Albert Camus said, *An intellectual is someone whose mind watches itself*. Not so different, surely, from Bresson's notion of directing one's self.

My suggestion that a director should be "mischievous" might seem irresponsible, but mischief is a vital facet in the crafts of story-making and storytelling. Going hand in hand with the need for a director to be inventive, both practically and creatively, this mischief—even while it eschews much of common thinking—has to function, has to *work*. Yet the word "mischief" might suggest immaturity, even naivete.

To say that the self of a director must be both experienced and naive might seem nonsensical. Yet there has to be something of the child in the director's self and surely in that of any artist. The all-knowing directing self precludes invention and mischief, and in adhering to the assumptions of common thinking can offer only the regurgitation of what has come before.

The experienced self is aware of *not* knowing everything and of making a virtue of this. The experienced self, while familiar with the success or failure of past approaches, leaves room for innovation. This entails a degree of naivete. The two facets are not contradictory, but work together.

The experienced self, of course, is very much derived from one's previous practice in filmmaking and the lessons learned, while also embracing the truth that every new encounter with the process offers more to learn.

The creative vision that comes from the self—which many regard as being too nebulous a concept to take seriously—cannot be taught. The director may not even know it is there in their work, but the engaged viewer will certainly have a sense of it.

The *shadow* within the self, in the sense that Carl Jung defined it, is central to its creative power. This is the source of subversive energy to charge the director's material. Like the child in the self and also creatively fertile, it resides in the subconscious.

The director aware of their Zen will have a keen insight into these considerations, as they will into what constitutes the conscious and subconscious selves.

5
The Director and the Conscious Self

Elements that either inform or constitute the conscious self include:

Cultural background
Ethnicity
Education
Beliefs and Convictions (often derived from schooling)
Ethics
Politics
Philosophy
Sensibility
Limitations
Other Activities/Interests

Cultural background

No one is without a cultural background. For the director, this foundation is seminal to their choice of material, their exploration and articulation of it, and to the authenticity they find in it and bring from it. A director's cultural foundations provide a specificity to their view and understanding of humanity, its interactions, its engagement with the world, its commonality, its spectrum of behavior, its soul.

A director's sense of story and storytelling will derive extensively from their cultural background. For example, an American filmmaker steeped in the adversarial individualism of their nation, and the imperative for agency this demands of the individual, may tend to emphasize the struggle of a character to overcome their circumstances and defeat their adversaries.

Because of the fragility of a relatively young culture such as that of the U.S., an American filmmaker may see life in a different light from the perspective of one from an older culture who might have a greater sense of community, of family, of duty and obligations to others, of tradition, and of the limitations of the individual's power in the face of fate and the universe.

To the American director, *conflict* may well be predominant in their grasp of narrative. Others might find their selves tied more to *friction*, or to *tension*, maybe to a "vibe" that can hold an audience—whether through wonder or mystery or something ineffable.

Filmmakers from across the world, though, will frequently imbue their narratives with a strong sense of precarity—in its direction, situations, characters, perhaps even in a film's visual language and style. A feeling of fragility, a danger of things falling apart, can lend a film its energy and life.

A sense of structure might also derive from a filmmaker's cultural/national background. Again, the U.S. stands out because of its origins in the latter half of the eighteenth century, an "age of reason" claiming itself as "enlightenment" and built on foundations of structure. In its political organization, its sports, and its approach to dramatic narrative, American function and practice are firmly rooted in the concept of structure.

Many American directors and writers might build their material around the template of structure, while those from elsewhere might find the nature of a film's structure from *within* its narrative.

As an educator in a graduate directing program, I gained enormous benefit from the different cultural perspectives brought by students from across the world and their often contrasting comprehension of life. With the class recognizing this diversity, the students were able to learn from each other. They also gained a keen sense of their own acculturation and of both its advantages and limitations.

Ethnicity

The ethnicity of a filmmaker may bring with it the foundations of culture, custom, and tradition, the context of history—social, political, international. It may perhaps also bring an understanding of the effects of a society's—and indeed the world's—hierarchy of power and opportunity, for better or worse, on one's community past and present. (Those of traditionally oppressed ethnicities may, through necessity, possess a deeper awareness of such things than those from advantaged peoples.)

Aspiring filmmakers once excluded from Western filmmaking because of their ethnicity may now find different opportunities, to a greater or lesser extent, than their predecessors. Those in such circumstances enrich and deepen the art of cinema while giving address to voices previously denied.

Education

The nature and extent of a director's education, as with anyone's, form an important part of their conscious self. This is not to suggest that academic success necessarily bears any relation to the quality or merit of their work. There may be a connection between formal education and directing, or there may not.

Some directors have studied or worked in the theater, as actors or directors; others have had no such grounding. Some have attended film school or learned their craft through work in production, while others have come to filmmaking by entirely different routes. Some have benefited from formal schooling; others have been self-taught or shaped by the lessons of experience. A few have drawn on all three paths.

Many directors will have had mentors of one kind or another—sometimes fellow directors, and seasoned ones at that; sometimes not filmmakers at all but figures whose cross-disciplinary insight offered a broader kind of wisdom. Most directors are aware of the influence such mentors have had, though the best of them leave their mark more deeply, within the subconscious self of the student, where their impact is often most profound.

Mentors, teachers, and educators in general may of course also limit the self of a student. They may have imparted flawed agendas, insisted on rules rather than principles, hard and fast answers instead of challenging questions. They may have imposed their own limitations, their own mindset, even defensive habits.

Directors benefit from the best possible understanding of their mentors and their education in general so as to take what is helpful while putting aside that which is not.

Beliefs and Convictions

Awareness of one's beliefs and convictions as elements of the conscious self is vital to the functioning director. Taking them for granted or not reflecting on them at all can lead to the making of films that proselytize rather than challenge. A director who seeks to champion their own convictions unquestioningly, knowing full well that audiences will happily applaud the moral message they receive, does nothing but reinforce the complacency and self-righteousness of the crowd.

The filmmaker who, on the contrary, challenges not only their preconceptions but questions their most deeply held convictions and brings this friction into their material, is more likely to arrive at fresh, surprising, and thus compelling work.

Certainty leads to dull stories and storytelling. Uncertainty is the stuff of tension and drama. The director should not feel too comfortable with their film as they are making it, so that they are able to have a continuing dialogue with it. They should listen to what their film is saying to them. They may not like what they hear, but their duty is to their film and to what it needs to become, not to the fortification of personal tenets.

This is not to say a filmmaker cannot be passionate about their convictions or driven by a cause. But that passion must accommodate contradiction and fallibility—the doubt and vulnerability present even in those who act with the best of intentions.

Ethics

Innately connected with a director's cultural background, beliefs and convictions comes their sense of ethics. How much of this is related to the conscious self and how much might prove to be inherent in the subconscious, and in the collective subconscious at that, is beyond the scope of this book. Suffice it to say that a director might do well to be aware of their ethical precepts and how they bear on their engagement with their material, with those with whom they work, and with their relationship with their self.

If Ernest Hemingway reflected that *A writer without a sense of justice and of injustice would be better off editing the yearbook of a school for excep-*

tional children than writing novels, the same might be said of the director.

This is not to suggest that the filmmaker should moralize through their material, but rather that, whether justice prevails in a story or not, most people—unless they are sociopaths—possess some sense of it: perhaps misguided, perhaps deeply considered, but in any case central to their connection with the human world. Although in the darkest noir, justice might seem absent from a film's milieu and the outcome of its actions, the sense of that absence might be thought of, in a way, as a presence. Not easy maybe for the morally aware director to deal with, but all the better for that. The filmmaker seeks not to soothe but to explore and reveal, however uncomfortable that journey might be.

In regard to their collaborative team, a director has to motivate and prompt colleagues to discover new possibilities and solutions. There is an art to this that eschews coercion and accords respect to both director and collaborator. Thus the director need not betray their ethical sense of how they treat others in order to drive the production.

Without an awareness of ethics, both collective and individual, we find it difficult to gather a sense of meaning, incomplete, paradoxical, and elusive as this may prove. The director is better off not sacrificing this vital sense, and, in effect, their self, in the process of making their film.

Politics

Many filmmakers are motivated by strong political convictions and bring these to their work to powerful effect, whether in the context of overtly political drama, in dramatic intrigue, or in the nuances of work less obviously informed by political considerations. Without human complexity though, characters in any genre—apart from comedy (and especially broad comedy)—tend to come across as cyphers, and in political dramas tend to serve the proselytizing of their filmmaker.

If the Zen of the Director may seem nebulous compared to the specificity of political perspectives, the filmmaker can usefully bring its practice to bear on the focus of their political convictions, as manifested in their connection to their material, in order to guard against proselytizing.

Philosophy

The multiple meanings of this word are so considerable that, for the purposes of this chapter, I will restrict it to the director's perspective on cinema.

From the austerity of filmmakers such as Bresson and Ozu to the flamboyance of directors like Lanthimos and Luhrmann, from the formalist precision of Kubrick's ending of *2001* to the spontaneity of performance in Kazan's *On the Waterfront*, the philosophies that lie behind cinema cover a broad spectrum. For some filmmakers, they provide a driving force for their work, while others might discover them movie by movie, still others not considering any at all—as though they were an affectation rather than a core foundation.

A philosophy might be conscious—hence its inclusion here—but might to the contrary be unconscious. The filmmaker may choose to think about it, to formulate it, even present a manifesto (Dogme 95, for example), or they may be oblivious to its power in their work, whether quietly active or overarching.

The philosophy of a filmmaker toward cinema touches on their view of humanity, on their concern for the language and "practical aesthetics" of the screen, on the level or levels of their fictions from everyday occurrences to melodrama, from social realism to fantasy, and on the pitch and register of the drama they create and articulate.

Bong Joon Ho's cinema inhabits the terrain of flawed humanity, offering a satirical lens through which dark comedy and tragedy converge. A Ken Loach film with faith in humanity's essential goodness will offer conflicts that ultimately affirm the dignity of humanity.

The nature of emotion, its portrayal and the way it is communicated—whether through a "hot" or "cold" approach, an immediate or distanced one, whether direct or indirect—signals perhaps the most fundamental aspect of a filmmaker's philosophy. Often connected to their aesthetics, their sense of style, the range of tonality they adopt, the relationship of the filmmaker to emotion forms perhaps the foundation of their art and craft.

The director's philosophy may well be the consequence of their cultural background, whether embraced and articulated or whether they have rebelled against it. They may choose to make work rooted in a familiar social milieu or they may be equally at home working in social environments beyond their experience. They may focus on individual protagonists or on ensembles.

The filmmaker who feels enabled by the conscious implementation of their philosophy will derive an organic benefit to their work so long as its life is not rendered barren by dogmatic adherence. The filmmaker who by contrast prefers not to consider it may find that the motivation afforded by their material alone, and by their wish to tell its story, proves more than enough to breathe life into their movie.

Sensibility
A filmmaker without a sensibility cannot have a voice and can tell a story only in the blandest of fashion. One

who restricts their appreciation of other filmmakers to fellow travelers in terms of taste is unlikely to evolve as an artist. This is not to say that directors should compromise their approach or be constantly switching it in order to match their latest inspiration, but that they enrich their understanding of the medium and its multiplicity of vision with each filmmaker whose work excites them and which they come to know at profound levels.

The foundations of a cinematic sensibility may have been forged in a combination of early inspirations, one's social and cultural backgrounds, and contemporary tastes and movements, together with the artist's own indefinable creative soul. Ultimately, surely, it is a mystery how an artist's sensibility comes together. That's the beauty of it.

A filmmaker can know it in their self, though, by working with material and cinematic language that seems authentic to them, that *feels right*. Adopting the sensibility of another in order to bask in their reflected glory or to adhere to the latest style will seem to the honest filmmaker little but an affectation.

The realization of one's sensibility, an appreciation of the challenges to it, a belief in it but an openness to other successfully articulated work, can be a central facet of the director's Zen.

Limitations

Many filmmaking educators ask their students to consider their "strengths and weaknesses" with the intention that they work on their weaknesses. It might prove more productive, however, for the student to consider accepting their limitations as integral to the nature of their choice of material, of their craft, and as a key to the realization of their voice.

Susan Sontag wrote:

Writing means converting one's liabilities into advantages.

We might reflect that this can also be true for film-making.

While some directors prove masters of many genres (Howard Hawks, Billy Wilder, William Wyler, Akira Kurosawa are formidable examples), others, unless they are journeymen passing muster across the board, will find their territory within particular areas: comedy, noir, horror, social realism, romance, Westerns, action, period, war movies, sci-fi or fantasy.

Such inclination as to genre(s) applies further to all elements of cinema craft: tone, style, performance, camera, world and milieu, editing, and so on.

The task of the director is not to be good at everything or to be able to manage everything, but to know consciously what they are good at and to go with it, developing, honing, perfecting (almost but surely never quite) their craft and mastery in those respects.

Better to be a master of one genre than an indifferent jack of all trades (unless a director can get anywhere close to the aforementioned multi-genre masters.)

The director should see their limitations not as drawbacks but as the key to a creative agency that embraces strengths as virtues while understanding weaknesses as guidance in *not* going in certain directions.

This sense of practical and creative resources can be applied to the director's approach to particular sequences and scenes. Rather than leaving the formulating of the most challenging cases until last because they seem to suggest approaches and techniques beyond the director's abilities, the filmmaker, bearing in mind their strengths, should consider the *purpose* and *meaning* of a scene—its function in the narrative—

and how this can be realized by means that lie within their wheelhouse. In this way, seemingly insuperable challenges lead not to the half-baked filmmaking of imperfectly realized scenes but to creative solutions that often turn out to be better than what was on the page prior to this revision.

Broadening the consideration of limitations, the director should understand that were a filmmaker, were *any* artist, to be in a position in which they had absolute freedom and in which *anything goes*, the evolutionary nature of the creative process would be liable to grind to a halt. Limitations of budget, schedule, casting, locations, material even, present challenges that may seem frustrating, yet through the director's practicality and creative ingenuity can be rendered the conduits to superior work.

Other Activities/Interests

Some directors might have few interests outside of cinema, the need to make or find stories and put them on the screen in itself being sufficient to prompt good work.

Those who have other interests—cultural, political, philosophical, or even in areas seemingly unconnected to filmmaking—are by contrast well placed to nourish their work with the concerns and insights of these other obsessions.

They can prove invaluable during formulation. The development and evolution of narrative elements, pre-visualization, and soundscape can benefit immeasurably from the references that the broadly informed and culturally aware filmmaker brings to their process.

Through the Zen of the Director, the filmmaker understands their conscious self as a reservoir of resources to enable and enrich their filmmaking art and craft.

6
The Director and the Subconscious Self

A director without a subconscious self might as well be an AI "being" working from the regurgitation of precedent and rote alone. There can be no connection to, still less any revelation of, the human soul from a filmmaker devoid of a subconscious. Fortunately, none of us lacks this most profound element—which the Zen of the Director embraces wholeheartedly, enabling the committed filmmaker to draw upon it in full while acknowledging it can never be completely known, even understood. Its mystery is the source of its greatest strength.

Unlike the conscious self, its subconscious counterpart is harder for those of us who are not psychologists (as it perhaps is even for those authorities) to break down into a comprehensive list of categories. In incorporating their Zen into their process, though, the director would do well to understand something of their subconscious so they might be aware of how its agendas—many unrelated to any particular project they are working on—might be influencing, even determining their day-to-day engagement with material and team in ways not immediately apparent to them.

Decisions charged by irrelevant hidden motivation, rather than enhancing a director's voice, will surely damage the organic connectivity of their film.

At its most potent, however, the agency of the subconscious is central to the director's process and their relationship to their film. British novelist Hilary Mantel commented that the imagination comes from the gut—a practice visceral rather than emotional, and certainly not intellectual.

The artist is helpless in the face of this primal force from within that *demands* they create.

Some broad considerations as to the nature of the subconscious that we might explore are listed here—with the proviso that no purely reductionist approach to this most precious faculty can be entirely adequate:

1. Intuition
2. The Shadow, The Id
3. Primal Needs—Physical, Emotional
4. The Fight or Flight Dilemma
5. A note on "The Collective Unconscious"

1. Intuition
Ingmar Bergman:

I make all my decisions on intuition… I must know why I made that decision. I throw a spear into the darkness. That is intuition. Then I must send an army into the darkness to find the spear. That is intellect.

David Lynch:

It's a knowingness, a feeling and thinking at the same time.

Impossible, and counterproductive to attempt to analyze, intuition is essential to any artist. The director must have a sense of when it speaks and the ability to trust it. They should, however, recognize doubts and *feel* it is their intuition that is speaking rather than any imposter. (See Chapter Three—The Voices.)

2. The Shadow, The Id

If the creative process begins in the gut, what might be there to inform or subvert it?

Without becoming too technical, we can understand what Carl Jung described as the *shadow* as being the sum of all in a person's psyche they cannot deal with, recognize, accept, or incorporate, and so reject, deny, suppress, and project onto others.

Such elements will often be negative and without function in society, but may, by contrast, be positive and lost to a person's functioning self. A fearful person's shadow might have absorbed their capacity for empathy, for example, as it might leave them too vulnerable, while a latent artist who fails to become an artist might resort to confining their creative impulses to their shadow, in daily life despising those who have incorporated their true nature into their art and their careers.

Many buried elements, however, will have been negative. A conscientious carer might have a repressed inner abuser, a life-saving trauma surgeon might have banished to their shadow an inner assassin, a mountain climber an inner acrophobic, each confining such negative impulses to their inner darkness.

Aspects of their material the director encounters that fall within the territory of their own shadow may prove uncomfortable for them to work with, even unmanageable—at least for the filmmaker who remains unaware or in denial of this aspect of their subconscious self. The honest, open director, by contrast, seeing parallels between their inner drama and that of their material, will find this uncomfortable connection all the more profound as a source of creative energy, inventiveness, and authenticity.

Sigmund Freud's *id*—unlike Jung's shadow—preceded, developmentally, what he described as the *ego*. Lacking any moral aspect, the id, he believed, was the reservoir of the pleasure-seeking impulse of sexual drive and of the instinct for aggression.

Cinema is an experiential medium. It draws on the viewer's full humanity, from the raw to the emotional to the cognitive. Some filmmakers, some genres, will focus on one aspect more than others, but it takes the moralizer (not the moralist) or the proselytizer to render unacceptable and out of bounds all animal aspects of life in an attempt to teach the viewer a lesson. The filmmaker may be a moralist (many great ones are) but cannot make movies truthful to the human condition, its complicity and contradictions, while at the same time moralizing, while teaching the viewer how to behave. It doesn't take the incorporation into their process of the Zen of the Director for the filmmaker to understand this, but it will certainly be of help.

3. Primal Needs

Our physical desires—for sex, for example—contained within Freud's id, feed cinema a potent charge when incorporated into action and imagery on the screen. Since almost its inception, cinema has conjured the erotic, whether directly or indirectly, flamboyantly or obliquely. It may be peripheral, perhaps barely present in some movies, while central and celebratory in the illicit, perhaps fantastical, worlds of others. It may be central to the voice and canon of some filmmakers, while of minimal concern to others.

For many decades, the erotic was viewed—often spied upon—through the male gaze, the film industry long a bastion of men, and straight men at that, who shaped its culture and sexuality. In recent years, with the emergence of more female and LGBTQ film-

makers, the full richness of this deeply human force—
a source of creative inspiration and sustenance for
artists and art forms throughout history—has begun to
be more broadly represented.

One could argue that the experience of sitting in a
dark, cavernous space with others while watching, to
greater or lesser degree voyeuristically, often transgressive actions on the shifting imagery, energy, space and
light of the screen might itself be considered erotic. It is
certainly powerfully experiential.

While the director may work primarily with
emotion, using their instinct and intellect to reflect
and hone their material (but not to disempower it),
they need to be keenly aware of cinema's experiential
nature. They themselves need to *feel* it in their physical
selves. Cinema has the capacity to engage the full spectrum of what it is to be human. From the cerebral most
importantly to the emotional, but also to the neural,
visceral, sexual, and tactile. From angel to beast and—
most intriguingly—to everything in between.

The Zen of the Director invites the filmmaker to
embrace every facet of humanity as they work with
their material—to see how each element may complement, contradict, or even clash with the others. How
they might subvert each other. How they might work
under the surface of behavior, in the subtext of action or
dialogue, or how they might take control of it, wresting
agency from a character's better judgment. How they
constitute elements of character. How they inform and
drive different, contrasting genres. And how audience
members mirror them in their selves as they gaze at the
screen.

When a character wipes a layer of dust from
a tabletop, the viewer feels the sensation on the
tips of their fingers. When a character hangs by a
thread from a high building, they share their vertigo.

A setting of ice and snow leaves the viewer feeling cold. A sexual encounter, especially one taking place in the flow of the narrative, perhaps in a situation of dramatic stakes, effectively shot and cut, leads to arousal in viewers.

Human truth, above all, whether in a realistic or fantasy context, renders the erotic not pornographic but powerfully and dramatically charged.

Need leads to desire, which leads to longing. Cinema, like other functional and visual arts, meets this longing. It is often said that it does this in the safe environment of a movie theater or a room at home, but the psyche, the human soul, can never be completely safe wherever it might find itself and remains ever fragile. Film does not offer therapy, not by way of catharsis—at least in the sense of "purging" dark impulses—or any other means. At its best, it offers imaginative truth.

With the Zen of the Director, the filmmaker seeks not to soothe or reassure but to reveal the bewildering totality of our being, whether it be within everyday existence, at its extremities when this falls apart, or in the wildest regions awakened by imagination.

An important note here on set process. Although a scene may come across to the viewer as sexy, and intentionally so, it is far from the business of thrills as it is filmed on a set that is working responsibly. Respect for and collaboration with the actors, awareness of their vulnerability, collaboration with an intimacy coordinator, respect for the crew—a minimum of whom need be in the vicinity of camera and actors—and careful formulation, if not rehearsal for actual performance then for approach, shot by shot, angle by angle, can yield the very opposite in the movie. What was deliberate, even dispassionate, in the making of the scene on set can appear spontaneous, out of control, and wildly erotic on the screen.

At times related to the erotic, at other times not, is our primal need for physical touch, for physical contact. When hands touch, when fingers so much as brush against the hand of another, there comes a connection, perhaps tentative, maybe affirmative, that no dialogue, no matter how brilliantly written, can convey. Robert Bresson, in particular, was the master of showing conjoined hands, giving us unforgettable actions and images.

The interaction of hand and brain, and its impact on our developing toolmaking skills, might surely be seen as a driving force in human evolution. The manual dexterity we have, as opposed to the more restricted Simian grip of apes, offers a primal, physical interface between our interior selves and the world. The action of a character's hands can convey more than facial expression. It can communicate a subtext readily understood by the viewer, an emotional truth the character is concealing or denying in their self.

The aggressive drive, arising from the id, as Freud envisaged, one can argue is not a need so much as an impulse. Whether it is actually an imperative deep in us all, or simply a reaction to the adversity of others, or the mere fear of that, or solely a trait common to certain personality types is beyond the scope of this book. It has to be said, however, that aggression has no place in the Zen of the Director apart from in its place in conflict and drama, where in some cases it might be an essential engine.

What may trigger aggression in anyone, fictional character or living person, is the need for safety and security, and the consequent fear of *the other* and the threat they might be seen to present. In the filmmaking environment, dangers to the successful completion of a project in the form of circumstances, events, or people can come seemingly out of nowhere. The director has to be non-reactive in the face of these, challenging as this may prove given the pressures, uncertainties, personalities and politics, and constant obstacles the filmmaker encounters at every stage in the making of any movie.

The Zen of the Director eschews aggressive behavior from the director.

4. The Fight or Flight Dilemma

Deeper and more primitive in us perhaps, even than our shadow and id, is the fight or flight dilemma. American screenwriting teachers, their focus on conflict above all, might insist that a character — certainly a main character — should always opt to fight. Fight brings drama. Flight is boring. But is it? Flight to fight another day. Flight determined by moral considerations. Flight that reveals inner conflict. Flight as refusal to follow previous modes of behavior resulting in detrimental consequences to others, perhaps to the self.

If it isn't easy to make any hard and fast rules about the fight or flight dilemma in dramatic narrative, it's also foolhardy to offer such certainties as to how the director might apply this primal quandary to their own self and their process — both in relation to their art and to their engagement with production.

It's difficult to see how fighting one's material could be beneficial, but then neither would fleeing from its challenges and problems. At all stages, the director has to listen to what their film might be telling them. What does it need? Where is it uncomfortable with itself, even in pain because something in it is not working, does not fit perhaps, and is in need of revision or reformulation or reinvention, or even, when it comes down to it, deletion?

Rather than adopting the fight or flight mantra, the director with a strong sense and understanding of priority, of when an issue is best resolved, can work step by step throughout the entire filmmaking process, not fighting but not avoiding challenges either. Facing them, engaging with them, working with them, is what best serves their task.

When it comes to interaction with producers, creative team, crew, cast, the matter becomes more complicated. We will consider the dynamics of some of these relationships in Chapters Nine and Ten. For now, it should be emphasized that the director's duty has to be above all to their film. (The safety of cast and crew and all on set remains paramount, however. The filmmaker can never be morally justified in putting anyone in danger of any kind.)

The director should have a more comprehensive sense of the connective tissue of their film than anyone else. Equipped with this insight, their priority is to make the best film they can, a film that works as it needs to, a film that is true to itself and not to the vagaries of modishness or to purely commercial criteria. They may face pressure from those with such or other priorities to do otherwise but are duty-bound to adhere to their creative integrity, just as they should remain faithful to the integrity of their film.

That said, the director has to recognize they have a financial and budgetary responsibility to those who have put resources into the project. Organizational and timekeeping skills, together with an informed awareness of production processes, ensure that the filmmaker respects and works with everyone involved for optimum results. No fighting, no flighting, but collaboration. (See Chapter Ten—The Director and the Creative Team, also Chapter Two—The Director, especially as diplomat, politician, listener, persuader, parent, teacher.)

4. A note on "The Collective Unconscious"

Carl Jung posited this concept, by which "primordial images" or "archetypes" common to all of us emanate from a shared subconscious. According to Jung, such motifs or symbols, independent of any particular culture or time, inform imagery across the visual arts.

Cinema especially, as a narrative visual form addressed to audiences sitting together in darkness, would be (if Jung was right, and surely he was) among the most potent of vehicles for such primordial fare.

Much of this resonant pictorial currency will function subliminally—and all the more effectively for that. The viewer will grasp meaning and reverberations from what they see on the screen without the inter-jection of any intellectual faculty. While the director needs exacting critical resources above and beyond those of the viewer (who may of course be similarly or more deeply equipped), their own subconscious—both individual and collective—is sacrosanct in the creative process. They don't need to analyze theoretically all that they include in their visual storytelling. The reductivism of theorists such as Joseph Campbell, for example, serves only to render mystery as banality, and human imagination as a rational, mechanical process.

The filmmaker, aware of the Zen of the Director, does not dictate their art, they *participate* in it.

To conclude, the director in touch with their own full and deep humanity—both that which is special to them, and all that lies beyond their acculturation and is common to people the world over, no matter their soci-etal universe—finds their self in a place in which they can be engaged most comprehensively and produc-tively with their material, with their self, and with their collaborators.

They may not be at ease with their story and its characters, and indeed may suffer inner turmoil in engaging with them. Acceptance does not mean peace though. David Lynch meditated, but we would never know it, given the intensity of the drama of his movies, in which he insisted there should be dramatic turbulence. Other filmmakers may have been less "enlightened," but have brought their fears and desires successfully to the screen.

The Zen of the Director does not ask the filmmaker to realize some perfect measure of personal holistic balance, only to bring all that is authentic in themselves—whether they are comfortable with it or not—into their filmmaking process.

7
The Director and "Territory"

Humans are territorial primates. Our sense of domains and boundaries, whether spatial or psychological, operational or emotional, actual or figurative — or some combination of the above — forms a deep currency for our interactions with the world around us and those in it. An important aspect of the Zen of the Director involves the filmmaker's conscious understanding of this territorial dynamic of human interaction as it pertains to their self and their work, and their ability to go beyond it in both areas.

What, in the sphere of filmmaking, might we consider the relevant territories? The following broad categories might go some way to offering a comprehensive picture:

1. The Film

2. The Territories Within the Film
    a. The Screen
    b. The Screen of the Mind
    c. The Soundscape
    d. Space and Boundaries within the Film's Fiction

3. The Director
   a. The Self
   b. Art and Craft
   c. Production

4. The Creative Team and Its Constituent Members

5. Personal Agendas

6. Cultural Assumptions and Norms

1. The Film

Without this overarching domain, all else is meaning-less. This is the territory that all other territories listed serve. This, above all, is the region that has to function properly. The film's *story* needs to be told, its *world* evoked, its *characters* realized, its *language*—formal, stylistic, inflected, uninflected, visual, auditory—have to be formulated and articulated, while its vision (should it have one, and should its filmmakers realize this aspect consciously or not) has to be realized and communicated.

The film, like its director, has agency. There is a paradox here, in that the director's agency enables them to understand and make the film, while the film's agency, through its challenges and insistence, draws in, drives, and even ultimately determines the successful director's engagement with it.

2. The Territories Within the Film

a. Along with story and creative vision, the address of the *screen* forms the fundamental territory of cinema. Images and action that play out within its frame, and those that do not, form its discourse for the viewer. The light, color, shapes, space, visual tones—what I like to collectively call *ikones*, after the Greek word for an image: εικόνα—the "flow of energy," and the editing form the language of the screen.

b. The *screen of the mind* is the territory a movie conjures in the imagination of the viewer. Prompted by sound, by elements outside the frame of a shot, by audience anticipation, by editing, and by dialogue, these *phantom images*, as Martin Scorsese has referred to them, can be more powerful than anything actually shown.

c. The *soundscape* of a film—its diegetic and non-diegetic manifestations, its score, its source music—form an auditory canvas, often subliminal, as emotionally potent as its visual counterpart, and equally cinematic.

d. The sense of physical *space and boundaries* within the fiction of the film as they pertain to its characters is an instrumental resource in the dynamics of staging. Second nature to director and cast, this can play out quite naturally, with modulation, as the blocking takes shape. Characters might have a "home" territory within a space, a composite space, an environment, or they may lay claim to one, which will affect their movements and behavior, as well as those of other characters.

The notion of boundaries and their effect on behavior is central. A character might be seen to hesitate to enter the physical territory of another—one they don't know or who is perhaps threatening—by stepping through a portal such as a gate or a doorway, or simply by coming too close.

This aspect of human nature and our relationships to each other and to objects of significance underlies much of the authenticity behind effective staging, offering subtext to action and dialogue.

In addition to the physical reality of space in a set, lensing has the agency to change the viewer's sense of distance and proximity between characters and objects. Two characters placed on the z (deep) axis within a shot will appear closer to each other on a longer lens (although the narrower focal plane may render one less sharp), but further away on a wide angle lens. This modulation can create useful subliminal subtext and tension—of intrusion perhaps, or uneasy proximity or emotional distance, a boundary crossed, or one established.

Space and distance within the fiction of a film, *as well as the passage of time*, are also mutable through editing, by which each may be either compressed or expanded.

3. The Director

The Zen-aware filmmaker understands the primal underpinning of territory and boundaries in their engagement with their material. Such things are instrumental when it comes not just to staging but in the collaborative processes of filmmaking, and also as the director goes about working within their own interior sphere.

The provinces, so to speak, of the director's territory might be understood as follows:

a. The Self

When asked if he felt less alone when making a film than when writing a novel or a poem, the Italian director Pier Paulo Pasolini said:

It's the same thing. Even more alone. Why? Because around me there is a lot of confusion. So the solitude becomes even deeper.

Discussed in Chapters Four, Five, and Six, the domain of the self is not so much a territory as a continent. The director should, somehow, in the midst of the pressured, highly complex, frequently unpredictable, physically and emotionally demanding, not to mention punishing journey of making a movie, try to find time to be alone. Solitude, the simple day-to-day activities of life, the moments of repose and reflection wherein one can take a breath — such things are precious. They are, in fact, indispensable, and very much a central facet of the Zen of the Director.

Sleep, pencil and notepad by the bedside for messages from the subconscious is one avenue.

Silence is another.

Another is favorite music for energy, reinvigoration, inspiration.

Or the company of loved ones.

The Zen of the Director welcomes these activities, which on the surface — and apart from the notepad at the bedside — appear to have nothing to do with directing a film.

Except that they do.

It is in this territory that the subconscious gets to work, that the creative soul and the challenged, pressured self finds sustenance.

As Pasolini noted, though, the activity of directing a film is in itself a precariously lonely one even if, one hopes, all around the filmmaker there is not so much confusion. Better to accept this loneliness, then, and even find solace in it, as there can be no creative agency without the spark from the director's soul.

b. The Art and Craft

The art and craft of the director lie in engagement with the material at hand: the film's narrative, its casting and performances, its storytelling, the cinematic language being employed, the film's style and aesthetics, and editing. They lie also in the filmmaker's collaboration in the creative contributions of their team: production designer, costume designer, cinematographer, sound recordist, editor, composer.

This multifaceted arena must connect function-ally with—but not be conflated with, or, worse, made subservient to—production.

c. The Production
While they should realize and utilize their position as the filmmaker with the most comprehensive grasp of the intricate connective tissue of their film and its making, the director also needs to be able to get the best of the logistical and creative abilities of their team.

These two distinct domains, art and craft on the one hand and production on the other, deserve their own brief chapter, which follows.

4. The Creative Team and Its Constituent Members
Within the territory of the creative team lie the indi-vidual domains of the specialized crafts and their practitioners. Each departmental head has to facilitate and oversee a functioning unit, both in creative and production respects. Each department has to function collaboratively with all others, under the leadership of the director, who motivates, facilitates, and oversees (although not by micro-managing) each department and their interaction with each other.

5. Personal Agendas
The soap opera of personal agendas—and the damage they inflict on a film and its makers—is anathema to the Zen of the Director. Power struggles, ego trips, and lingering resentments of every kind are toxins the making of a film can well do without. While an astute, supportive producer can help to temper these currents

and the territorial competition beneath them, the director—as parent, teacher, and diplomat—must set the example. For them, the film and its making come first.

6. Cultural Assumptions and Norms

These aspects of modish mindset are—like personal agendas—not so much territory as baggage. The task of the filmmaker is not to conform to some fashionable "conversation" but to step back and then go beyond it. A film may, of course, capture some element of contemporary culture without judgment or moralizing—allowing it to speak for itself—while the viewer, carried along by its drama, is left to reflect on its implications.

Worth considering, too, are the ways in which contemporary populist idiom frames thought and discussion, narrowing the space for fresh, original insight and understanding. When everyone on a team adopts the same expressions without reflecting on what they may—or may not—mean, assumptions easily go unchallenged. Shared idiom encourages group think and group identity. This is not communication but chorus, and thus an impediment to true collaboration. The director attuned to their Zen should take no part in it.

8
Art and Production

Many educational institutions that profess to teach filmmaking offer courses in "Film Production" that combine the artistic and creative heart of filmmaking with the industrial processes that serve it. This conflation is misplaced.

Yes, the director needs to be familiar with the multifaceted practices of film production in order to get the best out of them. They need to know *what* is (and is not) going on around their own efforts. They need to know *why* it's going on. They need to know *who* does what. They need to know *where* to turn, *who* to go to, which personnel, in which departments, when they need to make the most of their collaboration.

They need to understand and appreciate such things.

But the machinery of *manufacturing* a film is not the art of *creating* a film. These are two entirely different realms.

It may well be that many of the crew themselves possess considerable artistic talent and potential. Some will move into the crafts of writing, production design, costume design, cinematography, editing, sound, creative producing, and directing. Someone on set may make a comment the alert director might overhear and find of value, maybe great value. And it may be that, in the process of getting a shot, a crew member — skilled in ways the director is not — suggests something the director hadn't considered: a focus pull, for instance, or alternative ways of racking focus. Such contributions can help the director realize an intention through an approach they might otherwise have missed.

On the movie, however, art is not the job of production. Art is not production and production is not art.

Art reveals the human soul. Production does not. Production enables the art that reveals the human soul.

The film school that fails to differentiate between these two areas may give excellent education in the processes and structure of production in all its stages, but will inevitably be compromising their exploration of the level of cinematic art, its contradictions, its boundless canvas, its depth, its journey of constant discovery.

We can know everything there is to know about production. Few of us actually do, given the field's vast scope, but it remains a discipline that is clearly defined and learnable.

As with any art, we can never know all there is to know about cinema. The master director, therefore, is the finest kind of student — one who continues to learn. Like all true students, the masters refine and transform their art, revealing ever more of what cinema might be, though neither they nor we can ever fully grasp it.

When the two spheres, art and production, are treated as one, art is reduced to certainty, to only what can be known. The director is seduced into a fixed mindset.

Rules, regulations, must-do's and don't-do's confine the director to working by rote. The result is that films look, sound, and feel alike.

The blurring of lines continues long after film school, of course. It also affects those who haven't attended one. There's nothing more seductive than the camaraderie of the crew on a set, and especially on location away from home. A sense of common purpose, of mutual respect, is precious, buoying stamina during the frequently grueling days, weeks, and months of making a film. Without it, when there is tension on set, where there is intrigue, when grudges and jealousies play out among individual crew members and between departments, both production and direction become very much harder.

Camaraderie throughout months of production among its participants is to be desired and supported.

Without perspective, though, it can be problematic. Production is not there to serve itself. Production is the means by which a movie gets made. Crew members and the creative team need to engage with daily challenges. The pleasures of socializing that comes of this, of working together through the pressure of long hours, while enjoyable, are not the reason for making the movie. The movie is the reason for making the movie. It's easy to get lost in the subculture of production sociability and forget what is important.

An element of the director's Zen is the seemingly contradictory ability of the filmmaker to know and value the structure, processes, and social nature of production on the one hand, and on the other keep their self separate, to hold onto the loneliness of what they do. When the director works on the set, when they work in video village, it should be as though there is *nothing* in between those two places. No crew, no lights, no equipment, no cables, no distance between one and the other.

The director on set is in a realm of art and craft. Of camera, cast, story, emotion. All else is production.

The same is true of the broader nature of production—the movie business, the movie manufacturing and distribution and marketing business. (Although the latter are hardly "production.")

It was once said to me that because the term "show business" is used rather than "show art," the commercial activity of manufacture and distribution is what cinema is all about.

This is patent nonsense.

A film is not "product." It is not "content." *A film is a film.*

Within the framework of the Zen of the Director, the director knows, however, that to some extent or other they work in an environment without which most films could not be made, would not even exist, and so could not be seen without the business they feed. In terms of technology however, it is much easier to make a film now than it was as little as twenty years ago, and certainly throughout most of cinema history (although it seems more monumentally difficult than ever to get a movie into production).

Before developing technology made micro-budget film production possible, notable directors in the U.S., in Europe, and in much of the rest of the world—because they had no other option—made their work as economically as possible. Even so, it could prove to be expensive, and teams and crews, unless some were lucky enough to have a private income, would need some measure of compensation (which they still do).

The Zen-aware director works within the system or circumstances in which their movie can be made. They prioritize the integrity of their film, they challenge their enablers while respecting them. They have to be wily in order to deal with the many who have their own agendas and no interest in, still less understanding of, film. They should not, at the same time, exploit their crew or collaborators, expecting them time after time to work for nothing or very little.

With the mindset of zero compensation, filmmaking becomes the province of the privileged (as it has hitherto largely been—Werner Herzog, Martin Scorsese, Terence Davies, all from unprivileged backgrounds, being some notable exceptions).

Filmmaking, on the contrary, belongs to everyone.

It is up to the filmmaker to find the balance that rings true to their sense of their art and their sense of their self.

9
The Director and the Cast

Intuition plays at least as much an element of the director's work with actors as it does in any other aspect of their filmmaking—and perhaps more. No worthwhile director thinks, feels, or works in the exact same way as any other worthwhile director, even though they might share similar approaches and sensibilities, or be influenced by each other, or work within the same genres. (Indifferent directors, meanwhile, may ignore, not have access to, or even lack intuition altogether, working instead by rule and rote.)

The individual intuition of an effective director, when genuine, will be recognized and valued by the actor—for whom intuition is likewise the primary resource. From that shared recognition, respect naturally follows.

Not only are there are different schools of acting, but there are also different philosophies of directing the actor. Further to this, no two actors are the same. Any schematizing of the alchemy (which is in effect what it is) of the director-actor collaboration will always fall short without the enabling gift of intuition.

Whatever a director's way of working with actors, and however this may change according to the scene at hand, intuition has to play a central part in their interaction.

Some filmmakers allow the actor great agency. Some seek spontaneity of performance. Others — concerned with the precise granularity of a film's visual language, with the interfunctionality of camera, lighting, and mise-en-scène — will be more controlling. Some will follow a storyboard template but will want to work with the actor on the blocking of a scene before they can decide on camera placement, movement, and shot selection. Some will work with performers whose skill with the camera and lighting is seasoned and expert, while others might choose to go — or have no choice but to go — with a less experienced cast for whom any overbearing consideration of camera might prove intimidating. Other directors will be adept at working with actors at all levels of technical skill.

No approach is intrinsically superior to any other. From the actor-centric filmmaking of Mike Leigh to the aesthetic precision of Michelangelo Antonioni, who would instruct the actor in exactly how to hold the handle of a teacup,* the spectrum of the director-actor collaboration is both broad and contradictory. After his first feature, Robert Bresson chose not to work with actors at all.

Depending on the kind of film they are making, and on the particular nature of scenes and sequences, directors will often pre-visualize scenes — those involving stunts or special effects, for example, or those in which the story is to be told by specific camera placement and

---

* I heard this from Gianni Arduini, friend of, and 1st AD to, Michelangelo Antonioni on *L'Avventura, L'Eclisse* and *Red Desert*. He was also 1st AD to Fellini, Rosi and Wertmüller. I was fortunate to have him as my 2nd Unit first on *The English Patient*.

movement, but leave their final decisions regarding others until they have blocked with the actors.*

Many accomplished directors will assert that their most important task is to keep out of the actor's way. The most telling aspect of their work with the actor will have been their casting of that actor. The nature of a performance, of an actor's representation of character on screen, often depends, above all, on casting—one of Krzysztof Kieślowski's three most important factors in filmmaking (along with screenplay and editing, but not shooting!) Once that foundational decision has been made, the director would be wise not to force a performance at odds with the essence and nature of the actor they have chosen. In other words, keeping themselves out of the way. At the same time, they direct that actor's scenes through the balance of the director's and the actor's agency integral to the Zen of the Director and its absence of ego.

A further paradox in the director's work with the actor is the imperative for the filmmaker to find ways of challenging them in a manner that is stimulating, while at the same time being able to act as their protector against the machinery and processes of physical production. The set is a sacred domain. Actors need to be not only physically safe but emotionally secure from the busy production activity around them, its noise and interruptions, and its technical practices, irrelevant as they are to the cast on set.

These distractions can become exponentially more challenging on location—particularly when the creative rightness of a place has justified its choice despite the practical difficulties it brings. Yet the authenticity of a location—its limitations, its inconvenience, even its

---

* I was lucky enough to attend a Q&A with cinematographer Janusz Kamiński at AFI Conservatory when Kamiński explained that this is how Steven Spielberg chooses to work.

discomfort—may actually help a performer inhabit their character more deeply.*

If actors are to be open to the demands of emotional vulnerability that their craft, at least in various of its schoolings, encourages (if not in more Brechtian or Bressonian approaches), they must be afforded a safe space. Siloed from what at times can be intrusive production activity, they are better placed to journey into what might prove the uncomfortable, perhaps transgressive, offensive, and sometimes downright sociopathic depths of their characters. The actor enters a fictional world (but one resonating with their own non-fictional psyche). The crew work in a pressured, practical, day-to-day world. The director compartmentalizes, overseeing the boundaries but also the interfunctionality of these incongruous universes.

It can be helpful for the director to think of the individual realms of the cast and of the various departments as "bubbles." Each is special. The director interacts with each and, when practicality allows, implies invisible boundaries between them by physical proximity, by stepping away from camera or video village and onto the set, by stepping to camera or to sound, and by the volume of their conversation—loud enough to be heard clearly by those it is addressed to, but quiet enough not to be easily overheard by anyone else. This is especially important as it relates to working with the actors, often the most vulnerable of those on the set.

A director with a keen sense of their Zen will, through their behavior toward both actors and crew, convey respect for each while affirming the primacy of the actors' space both physical and emotional.

---

* Health and safety considerations, however, must never be ignored..

Finally, it's worth considering an aspect of the movie actor's craft that is not often reflected upon. I once believed that actors were not storytellers—that storytelling belonged solely to the director and editor. I was wrong.

The actor tells the story in so many ways. By looks. By actions. By body movement. By pauses and silences. By the way they convey subtext. An actor can tell what I like to call a micro-story simply by the changing nuances of facial expression:

They look.

They see.

They grasp the meaning of what they've seen.

They react.

They take a decision based on that reaction.

All of this can take place within a single close up, which can communicate more than dialogue ever could and prompt the viewer to understand its import through context as blinks, eye movements, and the subtle shift of facial expression articulate the inner thoughts and emotions of the character.

While this book is not intended as a manual of the director's craft, still less the actor's, at least in the technical sense, but rather as an exploration of the filmmaker's mindset—one that fosters awareness, authenticity, and effectiveness both functionally and artistically—it is useful to see how this micro-story from the actor illustrates our most fundamental engagement with the inner and outer worlds (apart from touch), and how it stands as emblematic of the director's Zen.

The interaction between exterior and interior— their osmosis and flow, step by step—can usefully be held in the director's mind as a point of reference when they are observing an issue, reflecting on it, and deciding how to act.

If the cast has its physical domain on the *set*, that world serves the domain of the *screen*. The flow of emotion on set—its theater of performance—may be more or less the same as its screen counterpart. Or it may not. It may be modulated, and considerably so, by editing, sound, and music, even by the reordering of scenes. (This latter can change subtext radically). The director, seeing their footage, may even find moments, looks, moves that took place before "Action!" or after "Cut!" were called. They may then use these when cutting together the scene, adding moments that fell outside the recorded action.

In recognizing the primacy of the screen (and the speakers), and the centrality of casting, the aware director should be diligent in watching possible choices for roles on camera, on a screen. Main characters who look too much alike and who are not stars or well-known actors might be confused with each other in the mind of the viewer. This deserves particular consideration in the casting of secondary or tertiary roles, where contrast or affinity of looks relating to the relative functions of the characters in the narrative might be of significance.

The director's Zen involves an awareness of all levels, layers, and elements of such multifunctional aspects of filmmaking and film.

To conclude, there is another paradox here—the paradox of the director's work with actors and their work for the screen. Paradox, however, lies at the heart of the Zen of the Director: not confusion or contradiction, but the coexistence of function and freedom in both the practical and creative realms.

10
The Director and the Creative Team

Who should be included in this category?

Screenwriter
Casting Director
Production Designer
Costume Designer
Cinematographer
Editor
Sound Team
Actors (see previous chapter)

Director and Screenwriter
The relationship between directors and screenwriters, or between screenwriters and directors (whoever might arrive first on a project), can be functional and rewarding, based on mutual respect and a sense of the symbiosis of the two crafts, or it can be distant, fractious, even fraught.

Screenplay, shoot, assembly, first cut, final cut are not successive manifestations of one unchanging thing but steps in the evolution of what a film is and must become. This is how the life of a film comes about.

Screenwriters who gain experience of the cutting room are best placed to understand this. Editing is a demanding, complex craft that is difficult to comprehend without having witnessed it.

On the other hand, the notion, held by some directors, that they must "make the film their own," without regard for the intricate web of connections a screenwriter has constructed, often leads to disaster. When that impulse expresses itself in ostentatious displays of craft unrelated to story, theme, or tone—a gratuitous "oner," for example, staged to flaunt imagined brilliance—the film is likely to collapse.

When the director is not the screenwriter, the relationship between the two will vary according to the nature of the production. In a corporate Hollywood environment, this may prove distant, perhaps even nonexistent. In other areas, more organic collaboration is possible. As with other collaborations of the director, a culture of questions, of the search for understanding, of a refusal to accept assumptions, and of the fearlessness of uncertainty—which both parties should be unafraid to embrace—allows for the evolution of the film along with the discovery of what it is.

The screenwriter does not have the gift of hindsight that the director does. This, directors should appreciate.

Some portion—perhaps more, perhaps less—of a writer's work consists of invaluable subconscious elements that seed the story but may not yet be consciously integrated into the screenplay. Directors need an acute sense of this, together with the skill of writer–director collaboration, in order to present their insight to the writer in ways that allow them the freedom to assess its merits. If the writer agrees, the director should consider whether these facets might be articulated on the screen or if the film would be better off if such things remained hidden, under the surface.

Both director and writer look for a film that works, for a story that both want to tell, and for a shared — or near enough shared — creative vision. Above all, they should be working toward a film that has its own integrity. By this, I'm not talking of any moral message, nor of any kind of formal or narrative perfection. I mean a film that is true to itself, however problematic, challenging, or inconclusive that self might prove to be. A film that is nothing less and nothing more than it *must* be.

It might seem odd to consider these observations when reflecting on the situation of the director who is also the writer. Yet this split personality scenario benefits hugely from the recognition that a single writer-director generally works in one mode as a screenwriter and in another as a director. (There are exceptions, for example Wong Kar-wai, who made *In the Mood for Love* without a screenplay.)

I first realized this during the making of *The English Patient,* on which I worked as Second Unit Director. At one point on location, before shooting a scene, director Anthony Minghella threw pages of his script into the air, exclaiming, "What was the writer thinking?" Yet Minghella was the writer. When he was writing, though, he was without the hindsight he found he had as the director.

While on the subject of screenwriters, it's important also to consider the co-writer-director dynamic. This collaboration can be its own check and balance to the dangers of ego over material, bringing the interior conversations of each writer into the conversation between both. The resulting to-ing and fro-ing, the back-and-forth, can be a catalyst for the productive evolution of the material.

Just as notable directors like Wilder, Antonioni, and Kieślowski worked to astonishing effect with co-writers, other filmmakers, like Hitchcock and Scorsese, have, in general, not taken writing credit. Yet, like the former category of filmmakers, they have given cinema their individual mastery and vision of subject matter, theme, cinematic language, and style. Not being the sole writer, in other words, is no disgrace for the director. It is the cinema they create that is the criterion by which they may be assessed.

Writer-directors who, by contrast, lack the contribution of another collaborator at the writing stage may offer some of the most potent of cinematic voices (Haneke, Andrea Arnold, and Bong Joon Ho are examples among many), while others, without engaging the doubts and challenges of the self, may at times lapse into self-indulgence—although how that might be weighed may rest on little more than the subjective judgment of the viewer.

Director and Casting Director

The director's collaboration with the casting director lays some of the deepest foundations of performance, emotion, and audience engagement. The art and craft of casting is central to non-documentary filmmaking. The director will have intuitive, objective, and perhaps experience-based criteria for casting options, but the specialist knowledge and insight a casting director can offer, and—quite apart from their measure of how an actor might relate to and bring to life a *main* character—their sense of which performers might be right for *secondary* and *tertiary* roles in ways that connect to central characters, may well prove invaluable.

The Zen of the Director can usefully come into play here, as the director will naturally be possessive about their casting wishes. This is all to the good. Very often, though, the filmmaker finds their choices unavailable, or unwilling to play a role, in which case the casting director can come up with alternatives and help the director with insight into how other actors might realize a main part, and which qualities in them might resonate with the character and vice versa.

Here, the filmmaker with a sense of the Zen of the Director may find their self somewhat less attached to preconceptions that are understandably so personal, given that people, their faces, their personae, and the nature of an actor's previous performances, prompt the filmmaker's subjective responses and instincts with such intensity.

The extent to which this attachment stems from time already invested, from ego, or from something functional, are questions the director needs to consider.

The casting director can be of telling support as the filmmaker directs their self here. Their collaboration can bring fresh and deeper understanding of characters and material when the director is, in Zen fashion, engaged with *what is*, and *open* to what may best be taken from it.

Director and Production Designer

Moving on to the creative collaborations that follow the director's work with the screenwriter and casting director, it makes sense to consider first of all the director's interaction with the production designer. Generally, it is this seminal team member who, before the cinematographer arrives, is next to come onboard.

The director's interview with the designer—much as with the cinematographer—benefits from an approach that lets the candidate articulate their response to the planned film before the director begins to outline their own. An interview that begins as a mutual exploration, yet one guided and subtly shaped by the director, can reveal insights the director might not otherwise have discovered. This can happen only if the conversation starts with the candidate's response to the material—to the story, the characters, and their world—and is not, at least initially, confined to questions of production design. The production designer is more than a creator of a film's visual world; they are a storyteller. Their work is not cosmetic but fundamental to the film's unity and voice. (This approach is also instrumental, of course, in revealing to the director whether a candidate might be right for them and for the film.)

The contribution of the production designer, as with that of any member of the creative team, cannot be organic or fully connect with a movie at any profound level unless it has the foundation of broad and deep understanding. Once director and designer have found their mutual insight, once the director has a sense of the candidate's intended approach, and once they are engaged, full attention can shift to the particular contribution of this collaborator in their department's particular sphere.

Locations, sets, set dressing—even possible vistas and wide "establishing shots" (I prefer the term "context shot," since it carries no presumption that it will necessarily start the scene)—require close, rigorous attention from the director–production designer partnership.

The director's work with the production designer is one of the most intensely important of their collaborations. It has to be grounded and thorough, in particular because once shooting has begun, the designer will often not be around, especially when the unit is on location. They may instead be elsewhere, attending to the next location.

Director and Costume Designer

The production designer may, on occasion, also serve as costume designer, though more often these will be separate roles. When they are, the director should ensure close collaboration between the two, while also giving due attention to their own relationship with this too often undervalued member of the creative team.

Vital in this latter process—and to return for a moment to the topic of the previous chapter—is the work between costume designer and principal actors. Given the actor's investment in the process, choices made with the participation of the actor, rooted in their intuition and insight into their character, can result in the more telling realization of a character on screen and, under the auspices of the director, to a stronger performance. With the involvement of the production designer, too, the orchestration of color palette, visual tone, world, and storytelling both on set and as they appear on screen, will be better coordinated.

This collaboration—between the director, costume designer, and production designer—should extend to the costuming of secondary and other characters, as well as to the wardrobe of extras. Unity of vision, while stemming from the director, finds wholeness in the combination of individual talents among the team.

Director and Cinematographer

The partnership of the director and the cinematographer can be one of the most challenging but also one of the most rewarding of the collaborations the director has with their creative team. The cinematographer, or DP (Director of Photography), is responsible for the nature and quality of the image on the screen. But the screen is the director's territory, too, their primary realm, in fact, along with soundscape and the "screen of the mind"—the images, often fleeting, that the film prompts in the imagination of the viewer.

Given also that neither director nor DP would be doing what they are doing without a degree (to say the least) of ego, their relationship can easily become competitive, leading to friction, conflict, and dysfunction.

What, then, can the director do in order to ensure that they and the cinematographer work together to optimum effect? How can they—Zen-wise—avoid ego and issues of the defensive and controlling self?

The director has to have the most comprehensive grasp of the connective tissue of their film. They bring the depth and breadth of this conscious insight to their decision-making process and to their engagement with their team. Even their intuition might be understood to work in coordination not only with their conscious insights but also with other subconscious activity throughout the making of the film, so that it proves more informed than if it were based on one-off "hunches." The director's art and craft is many-sided, many-leveled, eclectic, and expansive.

To an outsider, the cinematographer's craft might appear particularly specialized. With its strong technical bent, it can be daunting not only to the layman but the director too. One might imagine a disparity, then, between the defined boundaries of the DP's work and the multifaceted reach of the director's. Yet there is no reason to confine the cinematographer to the technical aspects of their craft.

The effective DP is an artist who brings to the film a keen, informed awareness of cinema—current and past—of art history, photography, story, and a breadth of cultural knowledge and insight. As the director formulates their visual approach, their language and style, they should involve the cinematographer in finding and drawing from visual references that might include other films (whether of similar or different genres), as well as photographs and paintings.

This shared exploration lays groundwork for the director to bring the DP into an ongoing conversation on story, character, world, tone, and structure, in which the director respects the cinematographer as both storyteller and artist.

That cinematographer will, in consequence, likely not be inclined to be overly protective of the boundaries between the crafts of the two filmmakers. When the director makes clear how they see their movie—what it is to become, indeed, *needs* to become—and what their intentions are in bringing this about, discussion between the two can proceed on this shared foundation and context, rather than veering from stand-alone decision to stand-alone decision on the part of one or the other.

But if the cinematographer is an artist, they are also, inevitably, a technician. Beyond shaping the light on a set, they must know which lights are needed and how to deploy them. They require a keen understanding of the physics of light, of lenses and lensing, and of the equipment that allows the camera to move in particular ways. They should be alert to the comparative merits of different camera systems. Once they needed a comprehensive knowledge of film stocks and processing; now they must keep pace with digital technology—a constantly evolving field that demands their continual attention.

While the director should be aware of the DP's skillset in these respects, they do not need to have as detailed a familiarity with all of its elements. When work between the two establishes, early on, a mutual understanding of intention, their decision-making, in consequence, will not be centered on the minutiae of technology or equipment but will develop organically, in connection to the nature and needs of the film they are making.

Some directors are more technically knowledgeable than others. In some respects, this can give them advantages over the less expert filmmakers, but it can also be a drawback. A decision made solely on the basis of technical specification—as regards lensing, for example, or exposure, or depth of field—without the grounding of what the shot is about, of the story that needs to be told, of the shot's connection to other shots in the scene, the act, the film, and above all the director's intention, can result in a choice that proves arbitrary at best.

So first comes the "what is this?" Then the "how do we achieve it?"

Some directors have a clear plan as to how they intend to shoot and cut a scene, while others want to block it out with the actors before deciding on their coverage. Some work in one way with some scenes and in another with others. Some work in both ways—formulating a scene in detail while still allowing for exploration with the cast on set. Some scenes—that might involve stunts, fights, special or visual effects for example—demand granular pre-visualization, while others, in which the drama is intimate and manifested in emotion rather than action, suggest a more spontaneous execution. Some genres, some budgets, call for extensive pre-planning, while for others, locking down the approach too early could signal a death knell.

Director and cinematographer need to agree on which approach across this spectrum is appropriate for when, for which film, for which scene. When other members of the creative team—the cast and crew—can sense, perhaps even see, this central collaboration working well, the director may find that all other collaborations proceed more smoothly.

Director and Editor

In contrast to the director-cinematographer collaboration—there for all to see, perhaps hear on set—the director-editor partnership is very much less in evidence for other team members.

I once watched an interview with Tarkovsky's editor—I think it was Michał Leszczyłowski—who was asked the question:

In a good film, is it the director or the editor who makes the cut?

He answered thus:

In a bad film, it's the director who makes the cut... Or... it's the editor. In a good film, it's the film that makes the cut.

In other words, it is in the cutting room that the film speaks for itself more than ever—although the astute director will have been watching and listening for its messages along the way. Not every movie is like a Tarkovsky film, however, while no director can be Tarkovsky 2.0. Some will have shot-listed, storyboarded, and formulated to the extreme. They will have planned exactly where the cuts should come. Even so, a movie's rhythm has to emerge from its shots and its sound, from its montages, from the variations of the takes chosen. A few frames one way, a few the other, perhaps, but the work has to come to life. It has to be born as a living artifact, no matter how precise the director's intentions.

The editor—and, of course, the director in their partnership—is concerned not only with making cuts or deciding where *not* to make them, but with working beyond the granular level to find the film's architectural cohesion. Editing, to be clear, is not only about deciding when and where to make the edit, it's also about bringing out the best, most functional story and telling it on the screen to best effect.

Structure (whatever form this takes), its proportionality and punctuation, is of fundamental importance. This will generally be evident in the screenplay, but when story comes to screen, a film's new manifestation requires further adjustment and honing.

A movie might also suggest that a scene may work more effectively when its place in the order is shifted. This may result in it taking on a new, stronger meaning than the writer and the director originally intended.

Such a process requires a highly functional, non-ego-based director-editor collaboration. One area in which the director needs to be wary of ego—and careful not to bring the baggage of the shoot into the cutting room—is in the handling of long dolly shots, or indeed any shot that may have taken an inordinate amount of time and effort to achieve. Painful as it may be to lose its beginning, to cut into it, or even, perhaps, to lose it altogether, the film is what matters above all. The expenditure of effort on set means nothing to the viewer, while a director's display of technique for its own sake, without connection to the integrity of a film, is of little interest to anyone but the director.

The Zen letting-go of the past and the living in the present, with what is, can inform this freedom on the director's part.

It should not be forgotten, though, that the director who wishes to be bold, who wants to make a bold movie, cannot afford to bow down to the strictures of visual expectations. They must take risks— although not without reflection, or without the faith that their intentions will come good. Creative process without precarity may remain a process, but is unlikely to be creative.

It is here that the editor, even more so perhaps than other members of the creative team, can prove the most useful check and balance for the director. With hindsight, reflection, analysis, and shared intuition, the two collaborators, director and editor, give birth to a film that since its initial seed of an idea has been gestating through each craft, each step, and each manifestation of what it has had to become if it is to work.

Director and the Sound Team

There are many technicians involved in the complex process of putting together a film's soundscape. From the sound mixer on set or location to the sound designer in post, and those multiple contributors—from Foley artists to music editors—who serve the latter, the director finds a different collaborative process with each.

During the shoot, when actors and camera are frequently the focus of attention, it's too easy for the director to neglect the sound mixer. This team member though has a vital role in the recording and mixing of both dialogue and diegetic sound and deserves the director's attention. The Zen-aware filmmaker, present in the moment, keenly aware of what is and how to get the best from it, does not neglect this technician, nor the results they are getting and the consequent implications for the coming complexities of post. The closest collaboration in the aural sphere, however—apart from that of the director with the composer—is with the sound designer. This is a truly artistic partnership. Cinematic soundscape provides verisimilitude, modulates the flow of emotion and tone—from reinforcement to dissonance—creates images on the screen of the mind, serves to give dramatic emphasis and suspense, assists in the determination of the viewer's "eye trace" over the screen, articulates rhythm, and can provide subliminal "messages" to the audience by way of sounds they barely notice because of their placement in the mix.

Unlike work with the on-set sound mixer, there can be time (if never entirely adequate) and space for the director to focus on their collaboration with the sound designer.

Summary

There are similarities and differences in the nature of the director's collaboration with the various members of the creative team. In each case, though, it might be useful for the director to imagine forming a "bubble" around them, a territory exclusive to the particular discipline, in which they are made to feel special (which they indeed are) and to be valued in accordance with their skills, know-how, and embrace of the filmmaking process.

It is down to the director's collaborative and leadership skills to bring out the best in each team and each team member. The Zen-aware director does not seek constant agreement, at least at the outset of the process, because we cannot collaborate with someone we always agree with. It is through the different perspectives the director encounters that they can crystalize and articulate their own vision. Indeed, it is healthy when the team comes to the filmmaker with their own ideas, and when the director can listen and learn from them—even if they are misconceived.

It is far more powerful to maintain authority by listening and navigating than by being an authoritarian dictator. Control freakery or micro-management robs the team of agency. On the other hand, films that work rarely—if ever—come about through committee. Collaboration is not a democratic process. The director has to be at the helm.

This can work only when the director fulfills their duty to communicate intentions clearly. Not only that, but repeatedly. Collaborators themselves have much to keep in mind and may not take in or entirely understand a point first time around, so may need regular refreshers and clarification from the director.

Constantly attending to the same issues, communicating the same things, bringing new challenges and approaches into the process, exercising patience yet driving the filmmaking all requires daily stamina on the part of the director. It is their care for the movie, their belief in it, and their need to bring it to life in the best possible fashion that enables the director to maintain this energy.

Through the Zen of the Director, the filmmaker incorporates what are often seemingly mutually exclusive facets of self and craft, and—rather than siloing them—allows for the pursuit of each so that, instead of fighting one another, they complement, inform, and connect within the complete filmmaking process.

11
Ambition and Awards

Ambition is the death of thought.

Ludwig Wittgenstein

The philosopher's adage would seem anathema to those attempting to succeed as a filmmaker in a fiercely competitive environment, one in which even the simple making of a movie—of whatever scale, genre, or merit—has become increasingly challenging. In this sense it certainly seems not to be helpful. The desire to make a film, to tell a story that means something to one's self and hopefully to the viewer, indeed to audiences at large, and to develop as a practitioner of the cinematic art, is an ambition no putative or neophyte director can be without. And with so many obstacles and so much pressure, it is the director's faith in their film—and their ambition to make it—that will see them through. Nor, in contradiction to Wittgenstein, ambitious or not, can they afford to stop thinking along the way.

The Zen of the Director, although it entails humility and a disengagement with ego, does not demand self-effacement or a lack of aspiration for the filmmaker's material and their chosen craft.

Yet ambition can indeed be a problem—especially when misguided.

The hunger for public approval, for accolades, for awards, for the colorful panoply of show business, has nothing to do with filmmaking. To see the process as going from idea to "red carpet"—as some teachers and practitioners appear to—entirely misses the point and badly orientates the aspiring director.

The occasion and glamour of a premiere or awards ceremony is not the destination towards which the filmmaker works, whatever the color of its carpet.

The final step is the moment when a film reaches into the heart and guts of the viewer. When it lingers—staying with them for years, perhaps a lifetime, passed on through generations—there could be no more remarkable destination. Posterity offers its verdict beyond our control. Better that the filmmaker, for the immediate present, focuses on telling their story and posing its questions.

A film may not reach into the heart and guts of every viewer, but will, in general, be better for that. This is not an elitist argument. It's not that there is some kind of league table of audiences. Directing masters themselves might highly appreciate a film that others among their peers criticize, and vice versa. Sensibility, taste, personal experience and development, for most of us, all come to bear on our engagement with films, although it is when one speaks to us through these layers, subverting them, perhaps, and connecting with our more profound depths, that a director gives us the most rewarding cinema.

The "red carpet" mindset, apart from relegating a film to little but the means to an end—art as the route to "success" and celebrity—invites the filmmaker to create work that meets general approval. Films, when well made, and when they conform to current causes and agendas in ways likely to pander to larger sections of the public, often bring widespread praise. Offering moral canvases so clear cut, they amount to banality, reassuring audiences of their righteous values, and so providing a route to the carpet.

It is the screen and its connection with the viewer that matters, not the publicity and events it may generate.

This is not to suggest that the director should ignore the financial aspects of a movie's production. While not aiming for maximum profit at the box office and after (maybe to the cost of the film's integrity), they need nevertheless to care that their film should not lose the investments of those responsible for its financing. They should, indeed, if at all possible, see it as their task to earn that funding back.

In parts of the world outside the U.S., where funding may come from institutions whose vision is more far-reaching—and more concerned with the development of the filmmaker and of cinema at large than with the short-term success of a single film— directors may feel freer to think long term and less about immediate box office. There are benefits and drawbacks to both environments.

To conclude, it's worth considering James Baldwin's observation:

The purpose of art is to lay bare the questions that have been hidden by the answers.

Yes. It is not to render the artist a celebrity. It is not to put them on the red carpet. In cinema, it is to reveal those questions on the screen.

Conclusion

With all that this book has explored, let's consider, with its perspective, how we might we understand The Zen of the Director.

Firstly, we acknowledge some fundamental aspects of the practice of Zen:

Living in the moment, in the present, openly, *working with what is*, while letting go of one's self and the assumptions of one's knowledge, in an emptiness for open and clear seeing—"sitting still," as it were, in a state of presence, of which one is a part, both engaging with the universe and connecting to deep consciousness, and the channeling of this as crafting the power of life.

This may sound overly metaphysical and too nebulous for the all-demanding, formidably practical, and broadly interpersonal activity of making a film, but it is not to be thought of as a moment-by-moment checklist so much as a foundation, reflected upon in rare but precious episodes of solitude, yet also underlying, and indeed serving as the means of, the most effective directing throughout the successive stages of filmmaking.

There is no single sentence that can articulate the kernel of this better than Robert Bresson's *The point is not to direct someone, but to direct one's self*.

The Zen of the Director offers insight into what it could be that directs one's self and into what it might be that can stand apart from the director's self in order to do so.

This ineffable agency can be appreciated and made active by the director's realization and assessment of, as well as connection and engagement, with the following:

The above understanding of the notion of Zen, and of how such an ancient philosophy might be relevant to the art and craft of the director.

The power and truth of intuition.

The voices that the director hears—directly, indirectly, strongly, faintly—internal and external, supportive and subversive, relevant and irrelevant.

The self in all its complexity.

The conscious self and the elements that comprise it.

The subconscious self and the elements that comprise it.

Awareness of territory as primal currency of human interaction, both internal and external, and how this relates to the director within their self, and to interaction with the material, the cast, and the creative team.

Awareness of the separate but interacting domains of art and production, the former never entirely knowable, the latter—a matter of structure, practice, and technology—while complex in nature and extensive in scope, entirely knowable.

The primacy of process over outcome or goal orientation and the understanding that the *creative* making of a movie is an evolutionary activity, one of discovery as well as intention.

Given this sense of how one might direct one's self, how can that directing of one's self then inform how one directs "someone"? And who, indeed, might that "someone" be?

There can be no adequate directing of someone without first directing one's self. That foundational directing has to be functional if the next step is to work to best effect. When the director successfully directs their self, it follows that their direction of others will greatly benefit. Irrelevant personal agendas will be avoided, mood swings tempered, questions, challenges, the search for insight and understanding prioritized.

This can facilitate the director's most effective collaboration—and symbiosis—with their material, their cast, and their creative team. In turn, these engagements may, throughout their work, loop back to bear on the director's directing of their self, for this foundational direction never stops flowing in both directions during the making of the film, but rather, continues until the final stages of sound mixing and color correction.

Even then, these principles may not come to an end but continue throughout the director's subsequent work—from their discovery and creation of their material, their navigation of the politics of getting films made, their making of those films and collaboration with actors and members of their creative teams in order to achieve this.

To direct a film, at any level, to any degree of accomplishment, is a remarkable achievement. To continue making films and to maintain such a career can be grueling indeed. The Zen of the Director, by taking the director beyond the limitations of their self, offers a source of sustenance and increasing insight to buoy and motivate the filmmaker as they go about their activity, and as they live their life.

Not doctrine, not dogma, not manual, not rigidity, not proscription, not cult, The Zen of the Director offers a wellspring of personal and artistic resourcefulness that embraces the creative and the practical, interior and exterior worlds, the realization of organic presence above the narrowness of self, and the application of this to filmmaking, both in individual and universal dimensions.

As this book demonstrates, the elements of the director's Zen are, moreover, already inextricably present in filmmakers and in the process of making films. The director needs only to bring this powerful resource to functional life for it to take effect as an invaluable companion.

Acknowledgements

The author wishes to thank Andrew Wagner and Stefan Kubicki for their invaluable guidance, without which this this book could not have been written, and to Paul Cronin for his crucial insights during this book's final stages and for bringing it into the world .

He is also indebted to his students of filmmaking who, over many years, have rendered this teacher of theirs a fellow student of cinema and its practice.

Sticking Place Books (stickingplacebooks.com) is a New York-based publisher specializing in cinema, offering interview books, memoirs, critical and historical studies, screenplays, and essay collections. Our titles include: